NEW DIRECTIONS FOR YOUTH DEVELOPMENT

Theory
Practice
Research

spring | 2011

Columbine a Decade Later
The Prevention of Homicidal Violence in Schools

Dewey G. Cornell
Herbert Scheithauer

issue
editors

Gil G. Noam
Editor-in-Chief

JOSSEY-BASS™
An Imprint of
⟨W⟩WILEY

COLUMBINE A DECADE LATER: THE PREVENTION OF HOMICIDAL VIOLENCE IN SCHOOLS
Dewey G. Cornell, Herbert Scheithauer (eds.)
New Directions for Youth Development, No. 129, Spring 2011
Gil G. Noam, Editor-in-Chief
This is a peer-reviewed journal.

Microfilm copies of issues and articles are available in 16mm and 35mm, as well as microfiche in 105mm, through University Microfilms Inc., 300 North Zeeb Road, Ann Arbor, MI 48106-1346.

New Directions for Youth Development is indexed in Academic Search (EBSCO), Academic Search Premier (EBSCO), Contents Pages in Education (T&F), Current Abstracts (EBSCO), Educational Research Abstracts Online (T&F), EMBASE/Excerpta Medica (Elsevier), ERIC Database (Education Resources Information Center), Index Medicus/MEDLINE/PubMed (NLM), MEDLINE/PubMed (NLM), SoclNDEX (EBSCO), Sociology of Education Abstracts (T&F), and Studies on Women & Gender Abstracts (T&F).

NEW DIRECTIONS FOR YOUTH DEVELOPMENT (ISSN 1533-8916, electronic ISSN 1537-5781) is part of the Jossey-Bass Psychology Series and is published quarterly by Wiley Subscription Services, Inc., A Wiley Company, at Jossey-Bass, 989 Market Street, San Francisco, CA 94103-1741. POSTMASTER: Send address changes to New Directions for Youth Development, Jossey-Bass, 989 Market Street, San Francisco, CA 94103-1741.

SUBSCRIPTIONS for individuals cost $89.00 for U.S./Canada/Mexico; $113.00 international. For institutions, agencies, and libraries, $265.00 U.S.; $305.00 Canada/Mexico; $339.00 international. Prices subject to change. Refer to the order form that appears at the back of most volumes of this journal.

EDITORIAL CORRESPONDENCE should be sent to the Editor-in-Chief, Dr. Gil G. Noam, McLean Hospital, Harvard Medical School, 115 Mill Street, Belmont, MA 02478.

Cover photograph by Dennis Caldwell and World of Stock

www.josseybass.com

Gil G. Noam, Editor-in-Chief
Harvard University and McLean Hospital

Editorial Board

Erin Cooney, Editorial Manager
Program in Education, Afterschool and Resiliency (PEAR)

Contents

Issue Editors' Notes

THE 1999 SHOOTING at Columbine High School is paradigmatic of a series of homicidal acts of violence committed by students in schools. On the morning of April 20, two heavily armed senior students fatally shot thirteen people and wounded twenty-one others before killing themselves. This tragic event received worldwide attention, beginning with live television broadcasts during the incident that included frightening scenes of students attempting to escape the school, followed by numerous interviews with survivors, grieving friends, and family members. Subsequent investigation revealed extensive planning and preparation by the two boys, who evidently saw their attack as an act of rebellion and a means of gaining notoriety. Writings and videos by the boys expressing their feelings of alienation and anger were posted on the Internet, along with many reports and articles offering theories and explanations for their actions.[1]

Many subsequent school attacks, as well as numerous threats of violence, have been linked to youth who expressed admiration for the students who committed the Columbine massacre. Homicidal attacks by students are not confined to the United States, but have occurred in more than a dozen other countries (for example, Argentina, Belgium, Bosnia, Brazil, Canada, China, Finland, Germany, India, Japan, Netherlands, Norway, Turkey). Understandably, there is international concern about school safety that has stimulated demand for new safety and security measures, as well as revisions to discipline policies and practices. The purpose of this issue is to describe the nature and scope of this ongoing problem, review relevant research findings, and identify promising prevention strategies.

NEW DIRECTIONS FOR YOUTH DEVELOPMENT, NO. 129, SPRING 2011 © WILEY PERIODICALS, INC.
Published online in Wiley Online Library (wileyonlinelibrary.com) • DOI: 10.1002/yd.382

We chose to focus on homicidal acts of violence by students (as well as threats to commit such acts), because these cases have tremendous impact on public perceptions of school safety and on school functioning (for example, an increasing number of students report not going to school because they feel it to be unsafe to attend[2]). We believe that these cases should be distinguished from ordinary forms of adolescent violence such as fighting and bullying that do not have lethal intent. We contend that understanding the psychological factors and environmental circumstances that precipitate these homicidal, and often suicidal, actions by troubled adolescents can lead us to viable prevention strategies.

Student homicides at school must be placed in a larger perspective of school safety. School shootings have generated public concern that schools are not safe for many students, but empirical studies show that school shootings are statistically rare and that students are at far greater risk outside of school.[3] School shootings in the United States actually declined following the Columbine shooting.[4]

There is a common misunderstanding that extreme acts of violence are so rare and unpredictable that prevention is futile. However, prediction and prevention are not synonymous, and effective prevention efforts do not require the ability to predict individual behavior. Public health and safety initiatives have reduced fatalities associated with problems such as automobile accidents and coronary disease on a large scale without the ability to predict individual outcomes. This issue identifies the emerging strategies for preventing homicidal attacks by students and provides information and insights from an international group of scholars and practitioners.

The first article documents the international scope of this problem and addresses some of the complex conceptual issues that make student homicidal violence difficult to define and study. There is no simple, categorical definition that absolutely distinguishes these cases from other forms of violence,[5] but there is sufficient consistency among them to conduct meaningful research on risk and protective factors that can inform evidence-based preventive models.

The second article presents two case examples from Finland that illustrate the interplay between the distal, international influence of the Columbine shooting and the more immediate impact of local peer interactions. The authors also point out the sequence of missed opportunities for prevention in the Finnish shootings that occur when a student is chronically bullied, develops serious emotional problems, becomes fascinated with Columbine-type events, and subsequently begins to discuss interests and even share with peers his plans to commit a similar act. These themes are echoed in subsequent articles and provide a basis for several kinds of prevention programs.

The third article explains the rationale for the Virginia Student Threat Assessment Guidelines and describes how multidisciplinary, school-based teams use a decision tree to take a problem-solving approach to student threats. The model takes a triage approach that involves progressively more extensive assessment and intervention according to the severity of the threat and the student's intentions. In most cases, threats are resolved with counseling and mediation efforts, and in more serious cases, the team must take protective action while simultaneously developing a more comprehensive safety and treatment plan. The author reviews two field test studies of the model, a study of training effects on staff attitudes and knowledge about violence prevention, and a quasi-experimental study showing that secondary schools using the model enjoyed a more positive school climate characterized by less bullying and greater willingness among students to seek help for threats of violence.

The fourth article describes a pair of prevention projects undertaken in response to a series of homicidal student attacks in German schools. Both projects examine the usefulness of a threat assessment approach to prevent violence by training teachers to recognize leakage behavior by students. *Leakage* refers to any behavior or communication that indicates a student is preparing to carry out a violent attack. This would include explicit or implied threats of violence, apparent fascination with prior acts of violence such as Columbine, or any evidence of planning or preparation to carry out an attack. The first project demonstrated the viability of training teachers to identify and report leaking behavior, and the second project—still under way—extends the first by training teachers on a larger scale to identify leaking and then having a school-based team evaluate the student and initiate appropriate interventions, such as mental health services, and in some cases, law enforcement action.

The next article describes the Swiss system of violence prevention through close cooperation of the judicial and mental health systems. Swiss courts, especially in Zurich, make extensive use of risk assessment and mental health services whenever there is concern about violence potential. The authors identify the 2001 Zug massacre as a pivotal event that increased court sensitivity to uttered threats of violence and present a case example of a delinquent youth who developed homicidal fantasies toward his therapist.

Although there has been little academic research on the impact of placing police officers in schools, this practice has grown substantially in response to school shootings and other violent crimes in schools. In the sixth article, an expert on the training of police officers to serve as school resource officers describes the challenges for officers and school administrators in working together and offers practical recommendations for the selection, training, and supervision of school resource officers.

There is widespread agreement that many school shootings could be prevented if authorities were informed that a student was planning or preparing to carry out an attack. A universal problem is that young people are highly reluctant to report on their peers. This code of silence[6] represents a major barrier to prevention efforts. The Colorado Safe2Tell® reporting system, established in the wake of the Columbine shooting, gives students an anonymous means of contacting authorities to request help for troubling situations. The seventh article describes how this system works, including extensive efforts to educate students and engage their cooperation that have resulted in thousands of reports and numerous successful prevention responses.

When authorities begin to consider prevention efforts, there are often questions about the etiological role of bullying, because so many of the cases involve youth who were victimized in some manner. There is also concern that these youth may have been encouraged to retaliate in a violent manner by their exposure to entertainment media violence. Similarly, there is apprehension that intense media attention to sensational cases might stimulate copycat crimes. The final article presents the thoughts and recommendations of a group of scholars with expertise in these substantive areas. Finally, there is a succinct summary of research on the frequent question of whether stricter laws or more punitive sanctions might deter youthful offenders.

Together, a decade after Columbine, these eight articles provide some clear directions for future research and development of effective prevention strategies for student-perpetrated homicidal violence in schools. Efforts to reduce bullying and be more responsive to troubled students offer a route for early prevention. More direct and immediate prevention efforts can focus on training school staff to be alert to student threats and other forms of leakage,[7] engaging students to seek help when they have concerns about the behavior of a classmate, and using standardized procedures to assess the seriousness of a threat and initiate appropriate interventions.

Dewey G. Cornell

Herbert Scheithauer

Editors

Notes

1. Erickson, W. (2001). *The report of Governor Bill Owens' Columbine Review Commission.* Denver, CO: The State of Colorado; Fisher, K., & Kettl, P. (2001). Trends in school violence: Are our schools safe? In M. Shafi & S. Shaffi (Eds.), *School violence: Assessment, management, prevention* (pp. 73–83). Washington, DC: American Psychiatric Publishing, Inc.

2. For example, Centers for Disease Control and Prevention. (2004). Violence-related behaviors among high school students—United States, 1991–2003. *Morbidity and Mortality Weekly Report, 53,* 651–655.

3. Borum, R., Cornell, D., Modzeleski, W., & Jimerson, S. R. (2010). What can be done about school shootings? A review of the evidence. *Educational Researcher, 39,* 27–37; Mayer, M. J., & Furlong, M. J. (2010). How safe are our schools? *Educational Researcher, 39,* 16–26.

4. Modzeleski, W., Feucht, T., Rand, M., Hall, J., Simon, T., & Butler, L., et al. (2008). School-associated student homicides—United States, 1992–2006. *Morbidity and Mortality Weekly Report, 57,* 33–36.

5. Harding, D. J., Fox, C., & Mehta, J. D. (2002). Studying rare events through qualitative case studies: Lessons from a study of rampage school shootings. *Sociological Methods Research, 31,* 174–217.

6. Syvertsen, A. K., Flanagan, C. A., & Stout, M. D. (2009). Code of silence: Students' perceptions of school climate and willingness to intervene in a peer's dangerous plan. *Journal of Educational Psychology, 101,* 219–232.

7. Compare Bondü, R., & Scheithauer, H. (2010). Explaining and preventing school shootings: Chances and difficulties of control. In W. Heitmeyer, H. G. Haupt, S. Malthaner, & A. Kirschner (Eds.), *Control of violence: Historical and international perspectives on violence in modern societies* (pp. 295–314). New York: Springer.

DEWEY G. CORNELL *is professor of education, forensic clinical psychologist, and director of the Virginia Youth Violence Project. He teaches in the Programs in Clinical and School Psychology in the Curry School of Education at the University of Virginia.*

HERBERT SCHEITHAUER *is professor for developmental psychology and clinical psychology at Freie Universität Berlin, Germany, and director of the Berlin Leaking Project and NETWASS Project.*

Executive Summary

Chapter One: Student homicidal violence in schools: An international problem

Rebecca Bondü, Dewey G. Cornell, Herbert Scheithauer

School homicides have been become a worldwide phenomenon. In the decade following the Columbine shooting there have been at least forty similar events in other countries. This article addresses the international scope of this problem and some of the complex conceptual issues that make student homicidal violence difficult to define and study. Meaningful research on risk and protective factors that can inform evidence-based preventive models is summarized.

Chapter Two: Cultural and peer influences on homicidal violence: A Finnish perspective

Tomi Kiilakoski, Atte Oksanen

Two case examples of school shootings in Finland illustrate the interplay between the distal, international influence of the Columbine shooting and the more immediate impact of local peer interactions involving both peer bullying at school and peer encouragement of violence through the Internet. Both cases involved emotionally troubled young men who identified with the Columbine attackers and aspired to attain notoriety through

similar acts of violence. There was a sequence of missed opportunities for prevention in these shootings that occurred when the student was chronically bullied, developed serious emotional problems, became fascinated with Columbine-type events, and subsequently began to discuss interests and plans to commit a similar act.

Chapter Three: A developmental perspective on the Virginia Student Threat Assessment Guidelines

Dewey G. Cornell

The Virginia Student Threat Assessment Guidelines were developed to help multidisciplinary school-based teams use a decision tree to evaluate student threats and take appropriate preventive action. A main goal of this approach is to allow school-based teams to recognize and respond to the developmental complexities of children and adolescents without resorting to the use of zero tolerance discipline. The model takes a triage approach that involves progressively more extensive assessment and intervention according to the severity of the threat and the student's intentions. The article summarizes two field test studies of the model, a study of training effects on staff attitudes and knowledge about violence prevention, and a quasi-experimental study showing that secondary schools using the model enjoyed a more positive school climate characterized by less bullying and greater willingness among students to seek help for threats of violence.

Chapter Four: Prevention of homicidal violence in schools in Germany: The Berlin Leaking Project and the Networks Against School Shootings Project (NETWASS)

Vincenz Leuschner, Rebecca Bondü, Miriam Schroer-Hippel, Jennifer Panno, Katharina Neumetzler, Sarah Fisch, Johanna Scholl, Herbert Scheithauer

Since 1999, Germany has experienced at least twelve serious cases of targeted school violence. This article describes two projects designed to fill the gap between universal prevention and emergency response in preventing severe forms of school violence in Germany. The Berlin Leaking Project examined the viability of preventive efforts based on early identification of leaking behavior that often precedes targeted school attacks. Leaking refers to any behavior or communication that indicates a student is preparing to carry out a violent attack. This would include explicit or implied threats of violence, apparent fascination with prior acts of violence such as Columbine, and any evidence of planning or preparation to carry out an attack. The NETWASS project will test a training program and intervention strategy based on those findings, examining the usefulness of a threat assessment approach to prevent violence by training teachers to recognize leaking behavior by students. This approach is extended by training teachers on a larger scale to identify leaking and then having a school-based team evaluate the student and initiate appropriate interventions, such as mental health services, and in some cases, law enforcement action.

Chapter Five: Procedures for preventing juvenile violence in Switzerland: The Zurich model

Jérôme Endrass, Astrid Rossegger, Frank Urbaniok, Arja Laubacher, Christine Schnyder Pierce, Konstantin Moskvitin

The Swiss legal system places strong emphasis on risk assessment and treatment of potentially violent offenders. Especially after the 2001 Zug massacre, there is close cooperation between the judicial and mental health systems to prevent violence through early detection and intervention. A case study of a risk management program for a dangerous seventeen-year-old delinquent youth illustrates this approach.

Chapter Six: The role of law enforcement in schools: The Virginia experience—A practitioner report

Steven Clark

Although there has been little academic research on the impact of placing police officers in schools, this practice has grown substantially in response to school shootings and other violent crimes in schools. With a standardized training program since 1999, the state of Virginia has law enforcement officers working in approximately 88 percent of Virginia's 631 secondary schools. Based on this experience, the state training coordinator describes how police officers should be selected and prepared to work as school resource officers. The success of school-based law enforcement requires careful selection and specialized training of officers who can adapt to the school culture and work collaboratively with school authorities.

Chapter Seven: Safe2Tell®: An anonymous 24/7 reporting system for preventing school violence

Susan R. T. Payne, Delbert S. Elliott

There is widespread agreement that many school shootings could be prevented if authorities were informed that a student was planning or preparing to carry out an attack. A universal problem is that young people are highly reluctant to report on their peers. This code of silence represents a major barrier to prevention efforts. In response to the Columbine shooting, the state of Colorado established the Safe2Tell® anonymous, 24/7 reporting system for receiving and forwarding threats of violence, bullying, and other concerns. This article describes how the program has grown to the point that it now receives more than 100 calls per month. A series of case examples illustrates its success in responding to threatening situations, including twenty-eight potential school attacks.

NEW DIRECTIONS FOR YOUTH DEVELOPMENT • DOI: 10.1002/yd

Chapter Eight: Recurrent issues in efforts to prevent homicidal youth violence in schools: Expert opinions

Karen E. Dill, Richard E. Redding, Peter K. Smith, Ray Surette, Dewey G. Cornell

Developmental research on social influences on adolescents can guide practices aimed to prevent homicidal youth violence. School shootings have repeatedly raised questions about the contributory role of bullying and entertainment violence, how news media publicity might produce copycat crimes, and whether stiffer criminal sanctions might have a deterrent effect. This article presents the thoughts and recommendations of a group of experts on these topics summarizing the current knowledge base. In brief, bullying reduction programs may be a useful early prevention effort. Television and video games with violent themes can encourage aggressive behavior, but these media can be used to teach more prosocial behavior as well. The potential copycat effects of highly publicized crimes might be diminished with more restrained reporting, although more research is needed. Finally, there is substantial evidence that increased criminal sanctions for youthful offenders have not had a deterrent effect.

School homicides have become a worldwide phenomenon in need of scientific study to identify effective prevention approaches.

1

Student homicidal violence in schools: An international problem

Rebecca Bondü, Dewey G. Cornell, Herbert Scheithauer

ON APRIL 20, 1999, two boys at Columbine High School in the United States attempted to set off a series of bombs and then opened fire on their classmates and teachers. In less than an hour, they killed twelve students and a teacher, and injured twenty-one others, before committing suicide. This event received worldwide publicity and became emblematic for similar shootings in schools across the United States. Student-perpetrated shootings in schools seemed to represent the high level of societal violence that is often attributed to the United States, but in the decade following the Columbine shooting, there have been at least forty[1] such events in other countries, indicating that the problem is not confined to the United States and deserves international attention. The purpose of this article is to define the problem of student-perpetrated homicidal violence in schools, to describe its international frequency, and to summarize the limited research on risk factors and prevention.

NEW DIRECTIONS FOR YOUTH DEVELOPMENT, NO. 129, SPRING 2011 © WILEY PERIODICALS, INC.
Published online in Wiley Online Library (wileyonlinelibrary.com) • DOI: 10.1002/yd.384

Definitional issues

The present article covers offenses with the following central defining criteria: (1) committed by current or former students (2) who chose to come to their schools (3) for the purpose of killing one or more victims (4) after a period of planning and preparation.

Various terms and criteria have been proposed to describe these cases: Most often, the terms *school shooting* and *school shooter* have been used to cover these cases because the defining features seemed to be a student using a firearm to inflict numerous casualties at school.[2] However, the choice of weapon cannot be considered an absolute defining feature of these cases because there are noteworthy cases in which some students used bladed weapons such as knives or swords, or even explosives.

There are also definitional questions about the location for school shootings. Certainly these cases received so much concern because they took place at schools. However, the definition of *school* is not as clear-cut as it seems. In the United States, for example, a crime that takes place while a student is traveling to or from school, or while attending a school-sponsored event, is legally considered a crime at school. Moreover, most of the literature on school shootings examined cases that occurred in secondary schools, but after the 2006 shooting at Virginia Tech, the category of school shooting expanded to include higher education settings. The inclusion of higher education cases led to further questions about whether crimes that take place in off-campus residences or near college property should be included.[3]

Another approach has been to define cases based on the motive for the attack and to exclude episodes of violence that seemed to follow immediately from an argument or fight. The U.S. Secret Service and Department of Education used the term *targeted school violence*.[4] This was restricted to attacks by current or former students using lethal means (such as a gun or knife), and limited to cases where

the student attacker purposefully chose his or her school as the location of the attack. Consistent with this definition, incidents where the school was chosen simply as a site of opportunity, such as incidents that were solely related to gang or drug trade activity or to a violent interaction between individuals that just happened to occur at the school, were not included. (p. 7)

However, it can be difficult to discern the student's reasoning and motives, and although some victims might have been identified targets of attack, in other cases the attacker seemed to have been indiscriminate in choosing specific victims.

In this article we use the term *student homicidal violence in schools* because we are interested in student perpetrators, and exclude crimes by school staff members or persons unaffiliated with the school. We make these distinctions because of our interest in developmental and peer group influences that seem central to understanding these crimes by young people. We are interested in both current students and former students, because their motives seem similar. Similarly, we include attempts to kill as well as cases that resulted in a fatality. However, our title is not entirely satisfactory, because we want to exclude some student homicides, such as impulsive, unplanned offenses that might follow immediately from an argument. In this article we consider only cases at the primary or secondary school level, and do not include cases arising in institutions of higher education.

The search for the one best definition and term for these cases is inherently problematic. From a broader linguistic and philosophical perspective, categorical definitions of natural phenomena can be surprisingly illusory, because many objects and concepts we encounter in daily life belong to fuzzy categories whose members share many features that are not necessary or sufficient.[5] Even ordinary categories like *student* and *school* can be difficult to define with perfect precision. Ultimately, the definitional issues may not be solved until enough research has been conducted to determine what criteria are most useful. In this article, we will use terms such as *student homicidal violence* and *school shooting* in the more general sense of a prototype case surrounded by other cases that are similar enough to be grouped together, at least until research gives us good reason to do otherwise.

NEW DIRECTIONS FOR YOUTH DEVELOPMENT • DOI: 10.1002/yd

The frequency of the phenomenon

Although violence at school has received great attention in recent years, it has a long history in Western culture. In *Centuries of Childhood*, the French scholar Philippe Ariès (1962)[6] noted that European school children in the middle ages commonly carried weapons and that many schools had explicit regulations banning swords and other weapons from the classroom. He cited numerous accounts of fights among students, assaults of school authorities, and public riots, many ending with fatalities. From this perspective, school homicides are not a new problem, even though the type of shootings seen in the past two decades seems distinctive.

The United States experienced a dramatic increase in violent crime, especially homicides, committed by youth in the 1980s and early 1990s.[7] However, the juvenile violent crime wave declined as sharply as it rose during the latter half of the 1990s.[8] Ironically, school shootings in the United States gained national and international attention and created a misperception of increasing juvenile violence at just the time when the opposite was taking place. By the time of the 1999 Columbine shooting, juvenile crime in the United States, including homicide at school, had reached a relatively low level, and has remained at this low level for a decade, despite the widespread media attention given to some extraordinary cases.[9]

Nevertheless, the Columbine tragedy has remained a prominent and influential event among American youth. Many of the students who subsequently planned or carried out homicidal attacks at schools referred to Columbine as a source of inspiration. More generally, after more than a decade, it continues to be commonplace for American students to make references to Columbine in making jokes and less serious threats, and for school authorities to worry that a troubled student in their school might be the next Columbine-type killer.

School shootings in other nations have also been linked to Columbine. Just one week after the Columbine shooting, a fourteen-year-old Canadian youth who had dropped out of school killed one

NEW DIRECTIONS FOR YOUTH DEVELOPMENT • DOI: 10.1002/yd

student and wounded two others in a shooting rampage at his former school. According to his family, the boy had been teased and beaten at school, and was stimulated by the Columbine shooting to seek revenge.[10] Investigations of European students who engaged in homicidal attacks at school in the past decade revealed their admiration of the Columbine shooting.[11]

The number of school shootings known so far may have been underestimated. Robertz and Wickenhäuser[12] reported 99 offenses between 1974 and 2006 and since then, additional offenses have occurred. Especially since 1999, school shootings have proven to be a global phenomenon. By now, reports about such offenses may be found throughout the world (for example, in Brazil, South Africa, Australia, Japan, China, United Arab Emirates, Finland, Sweden, or Austria; see Table 1.1).[13] Germany alone has

Table 1.1. Examples of student-perpetrated homicide in schools throughout the world after Columbine

Time, place	Offense
March 5, 2001 Santee, California	Student kills two persons and injures thirteen others
March 6, 2001 Limeira, Brazil	Student kills one student and wounds two others
April 26, 2002 Erfurt, Germany	Former student kills twelve teachers, one school employee, a police officer, and two students before committing suicide
March 21, 2005 Red Lake, Minnesota	Student kills his grandfather and his girlfriend, a security guard, one teacher, and five students before committing suicide
June 10, 2005 Hikari, Japan	Student throws bomb with nails and glass, wounding fifty-eight teachers and students
November 22, 2005 Nusaybin, Turkey	Student kills one teacher and wounds another teacher as well as three students
May 15, 2007 Maoming, China	Student kills two and wounds four other students
November 7, 2007 Jokela, Finland	Student kills six students, one school nurse, and the school principal before committing suicide
September 23, 2008 Kauhajoki, Finland	Student kills ten students and sets the school on fire before committing suicide
March 11, 2009 Winnenden, Germany	Former student kills fifteen people and wounds several others before committing suicide

NEW DIRECTIONS FOR YOUTH DEVELOPMENT • DOI: 10.1002/yd

experienced twelve homicidal attacks by students or former students since 1999.

Although the occurrence of school homicides in so many countries is troubling, it must be remembered that they are statistically rare events and represent a small fraction of violent crimes by youth.[14] Nevertheless, school shootings have a devastating impact on schools and communities, and have raised public concern like few other crimes. The reaction to school shootings has had a tremendous impact on school safety and security policies, as well as the everyday functioning of schools.[15]

Research on school shootings

Research on school shootings has been largely limited to studies in the United States and Germany,[16] the countries that have the largest number of cases. However, all studies have been limited by small samples with the associated methodological difficulties in measurement error, statistical power, and representativeness. Moreover, it is difficult to obtain detailed information on the background and history of these offenders, which is often either unavailable or legally protected. Therefore, some researchers have reanalyzed known cases or relied on media accounts, which can be unreliable and incomplete.[17] In some cases, media reports have proven to contain highly selective or even entirely false information,[18] and therefore are not a suitable basis for scientific research. For this reason, studies that rely on larger samples[19] or analyze a small number of cases in more depth[20] often come to divergent conclusions.[21] However, many authorities now agree that a single profile of the school shooting offender does not exist.

A further problem is that most studies lack comparison groups. The use of a contrasting group is necessary to discriminate specific characteristics of these cases and avoid the construction of fallacious profiles or warning signs. Lacking comparison groups, descriptive studies identify characteristics that may be common to these youth—such as being a victim of bullying and having a strong interest in violent video games—but are nonspecific and found in many other youth who do not pose a serious threat of violence. However, some researchers have compared these cases with youth who have committed murders in other contexts[22] as well as with youth who have made threats that they did not carry out.[23]

According to Kraemer and others,[24] risk factors and causal risk factors should be differentiated. Because of the absence of comparison group studies, the specificity and causality of risk factors for school shootings have not been empirically proven. So far they only describe correlations that have been determined retrospectively. Causality, however, may not be assumed. With these limitations in mind, there are some promising avenues for research and prevention efforts.

Threats of violence

One of the most commonly reported findings from case studies of school shootings is that many of the youth communicated their intentions. Threats may be made directly to the intended victims, but in most cases threats were communicated to third parties.[25] In their study of school shootings, the FBI compared school shootings with cases in which school shootings were planned, but foiled by the intervention of authorities. The single most important factor identified by the FBI in preventing school shootings was the reporting of threats by third parties (typically other students) that allowed school and law enforcement authorities to investigate and determine the seriousness of the student's intentions. Similarly, the U.S. Secret Service and U.S. Department of Education study concluded that schools should establish teams to investigate student threats.[26]

As described in another article in this issue, the Virginia Student Threat Assessment Guidelines were developed to carry out the recommendations from the FBI and Secret Service studies.[27] The Virginia guidelines establish a multidisciplinary team in each school that follows a decision tree and a set of procedures for investigating threats and resolving student conflicts and problems, such as bullying, that are linked to the threats.[28] A series of field test and quasi-experimental studies supports the use of the Virginia guidelines as a means of resolving student threats and promoting a positive school climate.[29]

Leaking

Leaking or leakage refers to behavior that displays a person's intentions. Criminal leaking occurs when a person intending to commit a crime reveals thoughts or plans to carry out the criminal act. *Leaking* is a broader concept than *threat*, although threats are one form of leaking. Intentions to commit a school shooting can be expressed through a wide variety of behaviors and expressive actions. For example, there may be statements that hint at an impending event or boast about the impact of an event on others. A student also may reveal violent intentions through essays written for school assignments, poems, songs, or drawings. Internet postings and chat sessions may be especially likely circumstances in which a student might express feelings of anger toward others, or even plans to commit a violent act. Leaking may also be expressed indirectly via conspicuous behavior patterns such as a disproportionate interest in topics related to violence (such as similar offenses and offenders, weapons, or war), or by suicidal thoughts.[30] Leaking is an important warning sign, as it appears to be less common and more specific than other hypothesized risk factors known so far,[31] is openly observable, and has been identified in every school shooting in Germany to date, as well as in many cases in other countries.[32]

The project Networks Against School Shootings (NETWASS) builds on leaking as a central warning sign and as an indicator for preventive measures. The project also tries to establish a procedure in German schools that allows for the identification and assessment of alarming behaviors such as leaking, a systematic search for further risk factors, and the development of suitable interventions.[33]

Leaking and threats may signal a problem that merits investigation; however, leaking and threats alone are not conclusive and must be considered in the context of further risk factors. Most importantly, they can lead to the determination that a student is engaged in actual planning and preparation to carry out a violent act.[34] As previous studies have found, student threats and leaking behavior do not necessarily lead to action. For example, a field test of the Virginia guidelines examined 188 student threats in thirty-five schools over the course of one school year, none of which were carried out. Ryan-Arredondo and others registered 202 threats during one school year among 160,000 students, and Bondü and Scheithauer reported 412 cases of threats of murder or incidents of showing off with weapons during an eleven-year period at around 900 schools in Berlin, Germany.[35]

It is important to note, however, that studies of leaking and threats only include cases that have been reported to school authorities. Many more cases likely pass undetected or unreported. These observations underscore the need to assess the seriousness of leaking behavior in order to justify further intervention. Some likely indicators that leaking is serious include the richness of detail, plausibility and consistency of the student's statements, and especially any behavior indicating planning or preparation to commit an offense.[36] However, as Bondü and others demonstrate, not every offender shows detailed and consistent leaking; therefore, other aspects of leaking and the student's behavior should also be considered.[37]

Risk factors

When there are indications of leaking or threats, a series of risk factors can be considered. No single risk factor can be considered conclusive, and there is no established formula for weighting or combining risk factors to reach a definitive conclusion. It is important to remember that any of these risk factors could be present in students who are not intending to harm anyone and innocent students should be not stigmatized as dangerous. Everyone engaged in the assessment of a student threat or leakage behavior has to consider the unique combination of factors and circumstances and make a reasonable judgment about the student's intentions.[38]

Mental disorders. The role of mental disorders in school shootings is not yet well understood. Most studies have focused on depressive symptoms, including suicidal ideation.[39] Others have hypothesized that students were especially prone to perceived rejections or failures because of an underlying narcissistic personality structure.[40]

Cornell and colleagues proposed that juvenile homicide offenders were a heterogeneous group with three main forms of psychopathology: (1) the largest group included youth with antisocial or delinquent characteristics who carried out instrumental crimes such as robbery; (2) the second largest group were youth with personal adjustment problems and depression who experienced a stressful conflict or problem such as bullying or abusive treatment that they attempted to resolve through reactive violence; and (3) the smallest group were youth with psychotic disorders who carried out crimes under the influence of delusional thinking and hallucinations.[41] Cornell applied this typology to school homicide cases, pointing out that the high-profile school shooting cases most often fell into the second and third groups, with the antisocial group receiving less media attention because their crimes were more easily understood and deemed less newsworthy.[42] More recently, Langman has similarly pointed to the potentially promoting effects of psychopathic and psychotic traits, as well as of traumatization, on school shootings.[43]

Some school shooters have also expressed intense fantasies of violence and themes of superiority and triumph over others. Such fantasies might be seen as compensations for negative experiences in their social environment[44] and fuel the planning of an offense. However, fantasies may be common in many students who resent being bullied or feel treated unjustly, so this risk factor cannot be considered specific to violent individuals.

Media consumption. The student's fantasies may be stimulated by intense violent media consumption and reports of school shootings and related violent topics, such as information on weapons and the construction of bombs.[45] The Internet provides a rich source of information on the details of prior school shootings that give them a sensational and notorious quality that can be appealing to troubled students.[46]

Negative experiences. Perhaps the most prominent risk factor associated with school shootings has been social rejection by peers.

NEW DIRECTIONS FOR YOUTH DEVELOPMENT • DOI: 10.1002/yd

Bullying, marginalization, or social ostracism have been reported in most cases.[47] However, some school shooters have not been mistreated by peers, and other negative experiences in school context, such as conflicts with teachers or poor academic achievement, can also play a role in the genesis of a school shooting.[48]

Stressful events can play a role early in the student's development of a negative orientation toward peers and school or serve as a precipitating event or final straw that prompts the decision to undertake the violent act. In these cases, the catalyst may seem like a relatively minor or insignificant event that many other students could tolerate. Some authors also report familial factors like parental indifference or neglect as risk factors for school shootings,[49] although the evidence for this claim is mixed.[50]

Access to weapons. Many offenders had access to firearms and often some familiarity with using them.[51] There is a mixture of cases in which firearms were purchased legally or illegally, or obtained from family members, friends, or acquaintances. In several German cases, the students resorted to bladed weapons rather than firearms, which probably resulted in fewer fatalities.[52]

Research on school shootings in Germany supported the presence of these summarized risk factors. For example, German perpetrators often had violent fantasies, showed extensive violent media consumption, and experienced serious losses as well as other stressful events shortly before the offense. However, there is also evidence for differences between cases from Germany and the United States. For example, nearly half (five of twelve) of German offenders were former students, and some had left school years ago. Also, there were more teachers than students who were victims of the attacks. These differences in the circumstances of the offense hint at possible national differences in catalysts and motives of German offenders.[53]

According to the results summarized so far, models that aim at explaining the genesis of school shootings should take into account a multitude of interacting factors. Only the interplay of personal and social factors in the long term, which is then further influenced by situational variables in the short term, leads to an offense.

For this reason, explanatory models focusing only on single factors (such as access to weapons, violent media consumption, or the gender of the offenders) are insufficient. Recent studies posit the role of multiple factors and their interaction over time. Some authors put special emphasis on negative social experiences and peer relations,[54] for example, in combination with intense media consumption,[55] or deficiencies in moral development,[56] which cause severe strain.[57] Other authors additionally stress the contribution of individual factors such as mental disorders, inadequate self-control, or maladaptive personality traits that interact with social factors.[58] However, all these models require more empirical support. As school shooters do not exhibit a consistent profile and the offenses appear to differ in etiology, it seems dubious that a single model will suffice to explain all cases.

Preventive approaches

Prevention efforts for any target problem or condition are often classified into three types of efforts: (1) *universal* prevention measures that provide benefits for the entire population; (2) *selected* prevention measures for at-risk subgroups of the population; and (3) *indicated* prevention measures for individuals who have been identified as demonstrating early signs or indications of the target problem or condition.[59] Effective prevention requires efforts on all three levels. Because school shootings are statistically rare events, intervention efforts at the selected and indicated levels are most needed.

Interventions aimed at a single factor are unlikely to be effective. Commonly recommended universal prevention initiatives, such as more restrictive weapon control laws, reduced media violence, and stricter law enforcement may be desirable from a general, societal point of view, but it cannot be assumed that any one of them will provide adequate protection from school homicides. Similarly, schoolwide antibullying programs and social competence curricula may have beneficial effects on students in general, but cannot be relied upon to eliminate the risk of violence.

Fortunately, the pathway to school shootings usually takes place over a period of months or even years, and frequently involves leaking, threats, and other risk factors. These observable indicators offer numerous opportunities for identification and intervention at the levels of selected and indicated prevention. Future research should be concerned with validating the most efficient means of identifying at-risk subgroups and demonstrating the effectiveness of selective prevention efforts. For example, the threat assessment approach as described in chapter 3 considers the complex interplay of personal and situational factors and guides a systematic search for behavioral evidence that a student poses a serious threat.[60]

In addition to selective efforts, researchers must determine indicated prevention methods for students who are identified as posing a serious threat of violence. The German Networks Against School Shootings (NETWASS) project[61] and the Virginia Student Threat Assessment Guidelines[62] are two examples of programs to identify and intervene with indicated students.

Concluding remarks

To conclude, student-perpetrated homicidal violence is a rare, but serious, international problem that is caused by a complex interplay of multiple individual, social, and situational factors. Despite the limitations of previous research, there are clear indications for future research, especially on the phenomena of leaking and threats of violence. Little is known about the specificity and predictive power of leaking and threats, and how these two overlapping categories of behavior are related. Are threats alone sufficient, or should school authorities pay attention to broader, but possibly more ambiguous, signs of leaking? How can schools encourage students to come forward with information, as the students are much more likely to observe threats or leaking than teachers? What are the motives for leaking and threats, and to what extent can these be regarded as cries for help or perhaps efforts by students to assess the response of peers to their plans?

There is a need for larger, more comprehensive studies that have access to more detailed information. It is also necessary to identify comparison groups in order to isolate specific factors associated with violent outcomes. How can we distinguish between students who make serious threats and those whose threats are not serious? And how do students who engage in attacks at school differ from other juvenile and adult offenders?

International comparisons could help shed light on cultural factors that lead to similarities and differences in offenses across national boundaries. The rapid advancement of international news media and immediate Internet communication with videos, personal Web sites, and live chatting has had a transformative effect on youth culture that has not been fully recognized. School shootings may represent one of the negative effects of that transformation and give us insight into other cultural developments that cross national boundaries.

It would be valuable to interview surviving offenders, including those whose plans were foiled, to assess their conception of their motives and to evaluate the presence of personality characteristics and symptoms of mental disorder, as well as their amenability to intervention and rehabilitation. Finally, although most studies have focused on the identification of potentially dangerous youth, there is much less knowledge concerning adequate intervention strategies. There is important work to be done on the treatment and follow-up of students who make threats of violence.

Notes

1. Bondü, R. (2010). *School shootings in Deutschland. Internationaler Vergleich Warnsignale. Risikofaktoren. Entwicklungsverläufe* [School shootings in Germany. International comparison. Warnings signs. Risk factors. Developmental trajectories] (Unpublished doctoral dissertation). Department of Educational Science and Psychology, Freie Universität, Berlin.

2. O'Toole, M. E. (1999). *The school shooter: A threat assessment perspective.* Washington, DC: Federal Bureau of Investigation.

3. Drysdale, D. A., Modzeleski, W., & Simons, A. B. (2010). *Campus attacks: Targeted violence affecting institutions of higher education.* Retrieved from http://www.secretservice.gov/ntac.shtml.

4. Vossekuil, B., Fein, R. A., Reddy, M., Borum, R., & Modzeleski, W. (2002). *The final report and findings of the Safe School Initiative: Implications for the prevention of school attacks in the United States.* Washington, DC: U.S. Secret Service and U.S. Department of Education.

5. Rosch, E., & Lloyd, B. (Eds.). (1978). *Cognition and categorization.* Hillsdale, NJ: Lawrence Erlbaum.

6. Ariès, P. (1962). *Centuries of childhood: A social history of family life* (R. Baldick, Trans.). New York: Alfred A. Knopf.

7. Cornell, D. (1993). Juvenile homicide: A growing national problem. *Behavioral Sciences and the Law, 11,* 389–396.

8. Cornell, D. (2006). *School violence: Fears versus facts.* Mahwah, NJ: Lawrence Erlbaum.

9. Borum, R., Cornell, D., Modzeleski, W., & Jimerson, S. R. (2010). What can be done about school shootings? A review of the evidence. *Educational Researcher, 39,* 27–37.

10. CBC News Online. (2000, November 8). *Boy charged in Taber shooting gets three years.* Retrieved from http://www.cbc.ca/news/story/2000/11/17/taber_shooting001117.html.

11. Scheithauer, H., & Bondü, R. (2008). *Amoklauf. Wissen was stimmt* [Amok. Knowing the facts]. Freiburg: Herder.

12. Robertz, F. J., & Wickenhäuser, R. (Eds.). (2007). *Der Riss in der Tafel. Amoklauf und schwere Gewalt in der Schule* [The crack in the blackboard: Amok and severe violence in the school]. Berlin: Springer.

13. Bondü. (2010).

14. Cornell. (2006); Moore, M. H., Petrie, C. V., Braga, A. A., & McLaughlin, B. L. (Eds.). (2003). *Deadly lessons. Understanding lethal school violence.* Washington, DC: National Academic Press.

15. Bondü, R., & Scheithauer, H. (2009). Aktuelle Ansätze zur Prävention von School Shootings in Deutschland [Current approaches for preventing school shootings in Germany]. *Praxis der Kinderpsychologie und Kinderpsychiatrie, 58,* 685–701; Borum et al. (2010).

16. Bondü. (2010); Hoffmann, J., Roshdi, K., & Robertz, F. J. (2009). Zielgerichtete schwere Gewalt und Amok an Schulen. Eine empirische Studie zur Prävention schwerer Gewalttaten [Targeted severe violence and amok at schools. An empirical study on the prevention of severe acts of violence]. *Kriminalistik, 63,* 196–204; Bannenberg, B. (2010). *Amok. Ursachen erkennen— Warnsignale verstehen—Katastrophen verhindern* [Amok. Recognizing causes—Understanding warning signs—Preventing catastrophes]. Gütersloh, Germany: Gütersloher Verlagshaus.

17. For example, Kidd, S. T., & Meyer, C. L. (2002). Similarities of school shootings in rural and small town communities. *Journal of Rural Community Psychology, E5*(1); Leary, L. M., Kowalski, R. M., Smith, L., & Philips, S. (2003). Teasing, rejection, and violence: Case studies of the school shootings. *Aggressive Behavior, 29,* 202–214; Verlinden, S., Hersen, M., & Thomas, J. (2000). Risk factors in school shootings. *Clinical Psychology Review, 20,* 3–56.

18. Langman, P. (2009a). *Why kids kill: Inside the minds of school shooters.* New York: Palgrave; Muschert, G. W., & Larkin, R. W. (2007). The Columbine

high school shootings. In F. Bailey & S. Chermak (Eds.), *Crimes & trials of the century*. Westport, CT: Praeger Publishers.

19. Vossekuil et al. (2002).

20. Moore et al. (2003).

21. Bondü. (2010).

22. Meloy, J. R., Hempel, A. G., Mohandie, K., Shiva, A. A., & Gray, B. T. (2001). Offender and offense characteristics of a non-random sample of adolescent mass murderers. *Journal of the American Association of Child and Adolescent Psychiatry*, *40*, 719–728.

23. Bondü, R., & Scheithauer, H. (2008, July). *Warning signs of school shootings and severe, targeted school violence*. Paper presented at the 18th World Meeting of the International Society for Research on Aggression, Budapest.

24. Kraemer, H. C., Kazdin, A. E., Offord, D. R., Kessler, R. C., Jensen, P. S., & Kupfer, D. J. (1997). Coming to term with the terms of risk. *Archives of General Psychiatry*, *54*, 337–343.

25. O'Toole. (1999); Vossekuil et al. (2002).

26. Vossekuil et al. (2002).

27. Cornell, this issue.

28. Cornell, D., & Sheras, P. (2006). *Guidelines for responding to student threats of violence*. Longmont, CO: Sopris West.

29. Cornell, D. G., Sheras, P. L., Gregory, A., & Fan, X. (2009). A retrospective study of school safety conditions in high schools using the Virginia threat assessment guidelines versus alternative approaches. *School Psychology Quarterly*, *24*, 119–129.

30. Bondü, R., & Scheithauer, H. (2010). Explaining and preventing school shootings: Chances and difficulties of control. In W. Heitmeyer, H. G. Haupt, S. Malthaner, & A. Kirschner (Eds.), *Control of violence: Historical and international perspectives on violence in modern societies* (pp. 295–314). New York: Springer.

31. Bondü, R., Schultze-Krumbholz, A., & Scheithauer, H. (2009). *Überblick Ergebnisse zu Teilstudien des Berliner Leaking-Projekts in Zusammenarbeit mit der Senatsverwaltung für Bildung, Wissenschaft und Forschung Berlin. Interner Bericht* [Overview of results from the Berlin Leaking Project in cooperation with the Senate for Education, Science, and Research Berlin. Internal Report] (Unpublished report). Freie Universität Berlin.

32. Bondü. (2010); Larkin, R. (2007). *Comprehending Columbine*. Philadelphia: Temple University Press; Newman, C., Fox, C., Harding, D. J., Mehta, J., & Roth, W. (2004). *Rampage. The social roots of school shootings*. New York: Perseus Books.

33. Leuschner et al., this issue.

34. Vossekuil et al. (2002).

35. Bondü, R., & Scheithauer, H. (2010, September). *Eine Generation von Trittbrettfahrern? Zu Häufigkeit und Merkmalen von Morddrohungen an Berliner Schulen* [A generation of copycats? On frequency and characteristics of threats with murder at Berlin schools]. 47. Congress of the Deutsche Gesellschaft für Psychologie, Bremen, Germany; Cornell, D. G., Sheras, P. L., Kaplan, S.,

McConville, D., Douglass, J., Elkon, A., et al. (2004). Guidelines for student threat assessment: Field-test findings. *School Psychology Review, 33,* 527–546; Ryan-Arredondo, K., Renouf, K. L., Egyed, C., Doxey, M., Dobbins, M., Sanchez, S., & Rakowitz, B. (2001). Threats of violence in schools: The Dallas independent school district's response. *Psychology in the Schools, 38,* 185–196.

36. Cornell et al. (2004); O'Toole. (1999).

37. Bondü, R., Dölitzsch, C., & Scheithauer, H. (2008, July). *Leaking as a warning sign in school shootings and severe targeted school violence.* 29th International Congress of Psychology, Berlin, Germany.

38. Cornell & Sheras. (2006).

39. McGee, J. P., & DeBernardo, C. R. (1999). The classroom avenger. *The Forensic Examiner, 8,* 1–16; Moore et al. (2003); O'Toole. (1999).

40. Twenge, J. M., & Campbell, W. K. (2003). "Isn't it fun to get the respect that we're going to deserve?" Narcissism, social rejection, and aggression. *Personality and Social Psychology Bulletin, 29,* 261–272.

41. Cornell, D., Benedek, E., & Benedek, D. (1987). Juvenile homicide: Prior adjustment and a proposed typology. *American Journal of Orthopsychiatry, 57,* 383–393.

42. Cornell. (2006).

43. Langman, P. (2009b). Rampage school shooters: A typology. *Aggression and Violent Behavior, 14,* 79–86.

44. Meloy et al. (2001).

45. Verlinden et al. (2000); Vossekuil et al. (2002).

46. Dill et al., this issue.

47. Leary et al. (2003); McGee & DeBernardo. (1999); Verlinden et al. (2000); Vossekuil et al. (2002).

48. Bondü. (2010); Hoffmann et al. (2009); Langman (2009a).

49. For example: McGee & DeBernardo. (1999); O'Toole. (1999); Verlinden et al. (2000).

50. Bondü. (2010); Hoffmann et al. (2009); Moore et al. (2003).

51. McGee & DeBernardo. (1999).

52. Bondü. (2010).

53. Bondü. (2010); Bondü & Scheithauer. (2008).

54. Leary et al. (2003).

55. Kidd & Meyer. (2002).

56. Thompson, S., & Kyle, K. (2005). Understanding mass school shootings: Links between personhood and power in the competitive school environment. *Journal of Primary Prevention, 5,* 419–438.

57. Levin, J., & Madfis, E. (2009). Mass murder at school and cumulative strain: A sequential model. *American Behavioral Scientist, 52,* 1227–1245.

58. Heubrock, D., Hayer, T., Rusch, S., & Scheithauer, H. (2005). Prävention von schwerer zielgerichteter Gewalt an Schulen—Rechtspsychologische und kriminalpräventive Ansätze [Prevention of severe targeted violence in schools—Forensic and criminal preventive approaches]. *Polizei & Wissenschaft, 6,* 43–57; Scheithauer & Bondü. (2008).

59. Gordon, R. (1987). An operational classification of disease prevention. In J. A. Steinberg & M. M. Silverman (Eds.), *Preventing mental disorders*. Rockville, MD: U.S. Department of Health and Human Services.

60. Fein, R. A., Vossekuil, B., Pollack, W. S., Borum, R., Modzeleski, W., & Reddy, M. (2002). *Threat assessment in schools. A guide to managing threatening situations and to creating safe school climates*. Washington, DC: U.S. Secret Service and U.S. Department of Education.

61. Leuschner et al., this issue.

62. Cornell, this issue.

REBECCA BONDÜ *has been the coordinator of the Berlin Leaking Project and is currently working at Ruhr-Universität Bochum.*

DEWEY G. CORNELL *is professor of education, a forensic clinical psychologist, and director of the Virginia Youth Violence Project. He teaches in the Programs in Clinical and School Psychology in the Curry School of Education at the University of Virginia.*

HERBERT SCHEITHAUER *is professor for developmental psychology and clinical psychology at Freie Universität Berlin, and director of the Berlin Leaking Project and NETWASS Project.*

School shootings in Finland have involved both peer bullying at school and peer encouragement of violence through the Internet, suggesting multiple avenues for prevention.

2

Cultural and peer influences on homicidal violence: A Finnish perspective

Tomi Kiilakoski, Atte Oksanen

TWO RECENT SCHOOL SHOOTINGS shocked Finland, a small northern European country with a population of 5.4 million. The young male adults, Pekka-Eric Auvinen (eighteen) and Matti Saari (twenty-two), committed two of the most severe crimes in the modern history of Finland. Auvinen murdered eight people in Jokela upper secondary school in 2007 and Saari murdered ten at a vocational college in Kauhajoki in 2008. Both posted statements and videos about their intentions on the Internet before carrying out a shooting rampage targeted at fellow students and school staff. Both committed suicide at the scene.

Lethal violence in Finnish schools is rare, but not unprecedented. Lone male students, using a spade and a knife, respectively, killed two teachers in 1981 and 1984. In 1989 a fourteen-year-old boy shot two of his classmates with a pistol in a Raumanmeri secondary school. Nevertheless, the crimes in Jokela and Kauhajoki

NEW DIRECTIONS FOR YOUTH DEVELOPMENT, NO. 129, SPRING 2011 © WILEY PERIODICALS, INC.
Published online in Wiley Online Library (wileyonlinelibrary.com) • DOI: 10.1002/yd.385

made school shootings a media spectacle and phenomenon in Finland. In the aftermath of these shootings, hundreds of schools received threats of violence.

In this article, we consider the cultural and peer influences on homicidal violence by closely examining the Jokela and Kauhajoki school shootings. We also make some references to the earlier Raumanmeri case. Pre-investigation reports by the Finnish police and the reports by the government commissions created to investigate the shootings provided background material. The police reports include descriptions of the events, previous behavior by the offender that can be linked to the shootings, and transcribed interviews of the eyewitnesses and other people involved.

Peer relations in Finnish schools

The Finnish school system is based on an egalitarian educational policy. All students follow the same curriculum, so that differences in economic or social capital do not limit anyone's educational opportunities. Finland has achieved considerable success in the Pisa studies (The Programme for International Student Assessment) by the Organization for Economic Cooperation and Development (OECD) in 2000, 2003, and 2006.[1]

However, a World Health Organization (WHO) study found that school satisfaction of Finnish children is lower than international averages in all age groups. For example, only 11 percent of fifteen-year-old girls and 9 percent of boys reported liking school.[2] One reason for this dissatisfaction might be the social climate in the schools. An analysis of the WHO data found that 28 percent of boys and 42 percent of girls in the ninth grade feel that peer relations in their school were bad.[3]

Several national studies show that bullying is a pervasive phenomenon in schools. In 2008, half (49%) of 15–16-year-old students reported that they had sometimes bullied other children.[4] According to the Finnish School Health Survey 2009, 8 percent of 14–15-year-old participants were bullied weekly.[5] Even more severe forms of violence are commonplace in Finnish schools. Forty percent of 15-year-old boys and 30 percent of girls report that they had been assaulted or threatened with assault within the last year.[6] Another study showed that 24 percent of 15–16-year-old boys and 5 percent of girls experienced physical violence within the last year.[7]

All three Finnish school shootings were associated with negative and violent experiences in school. The shooter in Raumanmeri (1989) targeted pupils with whom he had disagreements. He mentioned bullying as a motive and wanted to "eliminate" three individuals who were not nice to him.[8]

The Jokela shooter Auvinen had been bullied from the fourth grade, according to his parents. The teachers in the primary school, however, did not consider bullying to be a problem. His family relations were normal. His parents actively tried to solve the problems with bullying, although this alienated them within the local community.[9] Auvinen lived in the small close-knit community of Jokela, which has been described as a peaceful place where such a tragedy was inconceivable. Despite its image as a nice suburban neighborhood, Jokela was also known before the shootings for youth problems with drug use and bullying.[10]

The Kauhajoki shooter, Saari, had a complex life history. Before he turned eighteen, he had attended nine different schools and lived at twelve different addresses in seven different towns or villages.[11] His mother described him as being lively during his first years, but later shy, silent, and withdrawn. His parents divorced when he was three years old. His mother remarried six years later and family relations were seemingly normal. Saari was close to an older brother and deeply troubled by his death from a congenital illness when he was seventeen and his brother twenty-one. At school, other students bullied, assaulted, and spat on him, and he dropped out of upper secondary school. During his compulsory military service, he reported to the doctor that he had been bullied (for example, later, he told his mother that his military peers had urinated on his bed). He had reported sleep problems, anxiety, and suicidal thoughts to his doctor.[12] He was granted a termination of his military service because of bullying, mental disorders, and an injury to his leg. Around the same time, he became interested in international school shooting cases.[13]

Although there is no clear causal link between school bullying and becoming a school shooter, the Finnish shooters tended to feel marginalized and to lack peer group approval in their school careers. This observation is consistent with the link between peer rejection and antisocial behavior observed in other studies.[14]

School shootings often take place in rural and suburban communities.[15] A small community like Jokela is likely to have stricter behavioral norms and expectations than larger, urban communities.[16] Hence it might be a more vulnerable place for bullying and ostracism.

The Finnish shooters suffered from mental disorders that were not properly treated. Being a victim of school bullying might have affected these problems. A Finnish follow-up study found out that children who were bullied at the age of eight were more likely to have anxiety disorders 10 to 15 years later.[17] A Dutch research group also found that victims of bullying had higher rates of psychosomatic and psychosocial problems compared to those children who were not bullied.[18]

A school doctor prescribed Auvinen an SSRI (selective serotonin reuptake inhibitor) for panic disorder and fear of social situations in 2006. Later, less than one year before the shootings, his parents tried to get him psychiatric help. The Adolescent Psychiatry Outpatient Clinic, however, refused the referral, because Auvinen did not present with sufficiently serious symptoms of depression. The access to long-term therapy or psychiatric treatment is fairly difficult in Finland because of long wait lists and a shortage of providers.[19]

The first observations of mental disorder in the Kauhajoki shooter were made when he was thirteen years old. Saari's symptoms worsened during the two years before the shootings, especially after his failed military service. He experienced sleep problems, panic attacks, depression, and suicidal thoughts. He was diagnosed as having moderate depression in 2008. He scored high on an alcohol abuse screening test, and seemed to have a fairly limited social network. Saari was treated with SSRIs as well as a benzodiazepine (alpratzolam, also known as Xanax) for panic attacks, although he never met the psychiatrist who wrote him the prescriptions and was seen by a nurse.[20]

Peer relations on the Internet

Finnish young people spend approximately two hours per day on the Internet. Most (83 percent) use the Internet daily and 70 percent have published photos of themselves in net forums, such as Facebook or IRC-Galleria, the largest social networking Web site in Finland.[21]

Auvinen stands out as a remarkably active social media user. He used several nicknames and had multiple YouTube accounts on which he posted video material containing his own philosophical statements, sadomasochistic sexual fantasies, and homage to prior school shooters. He was a member of several discussion groups and net forums.

The net provides an arena for young people in socially marginalized positions to link up with new friends, but it can also lead to peers who might support or encourage fantasies of violent revenge. Auvinen was a shy and withdrawn person in his school. On the Internet, he had an aggressive identity that glorified violence, was interested in guns and murderers, and expressed an ideology that was a form of social Darwinism with emphasis on natural selection.

Peer groups identified through the Internet have played an important role in facilitating school shootings in Finland. One of the Internet arenas was a discussion group dedicated to the Columbine high school shooters. Auvinen obtained information about previous shootings and studied how they were carried out. He spoke with peers who shared his positive views about the Columbine shooting and directly or indirectly supported his ideas of carrying out a similar act of violence. One of the participants told the

police that she had two long discussions with Auvinen. They discussed their psychiatric medications, their thoughts about school
shootings, and his purchase of a gun.[22] Even if the Internet participants do not explicitly endorse an act of violence, their communications can be interpreted by a troubled youth as encouraging or
supporting his decision to take action.

Auvinen wanted his crime to receive public attention. On the
morning of the shooting, he made final edits to an Internet media
package that included his manifesto, pictures, and videos. He
uploaded the media package to rapidshare.com less than twenty
minutes before he shot his first victim.[23] In his media package, he
expressed his contempt for mass society and ordinary people and
stated that the shooting was an act of political terrorism. He
claimed to attack not only the school, but all of society and the
human race. His package included a manifesto where he stated
that he wanted to start a revolution. He did not blame people for
treating him badly on a personal level. Instead, he used existential
and antidemocratic jargon to justify his act and appeal to potential
followers. He wanted to "inspire all the intelligent people and start
some sort of revolution against the current systems."

Saari was also active on the Internet. He had four YouTube videos that showed him firing his gun on a shooting range and seven
photos of himself with a gun on IRC-Galleria. There are many
indications that Saari was influenced by Auvinen. He followed the
same procedure of leaving a media package in Rapidshare, entitled
"Massacre in Kauhajoki."[24] He took similar photos of himself with
a gun, visited Jokela, and photographed Jokela high school. He
ordered a handgun from the Web site of the same shop where
Auvinen bought his weapon.[25] They shared the same social network in YouTube.[26]

The Kauhajoki and Jokela cases suggest that the role of the
Internet and social media should be given serious consideration in
school violence prevention. The Internet has become increasingly
important to youth as a means of communication and self-
expression in the past ten years. Columbine assailant Eric Harris
had a Web page that he used to describe his violent fantasies and

threats.[27] Both Auvinen and Saari went far beyond that and used the Internet to publish their videos, to project a violent identity in their communications in the social media, and to distribute descriptions of their intentions just prior to the shooting.

Peer knowledge of the potential for violence

Both of the Finnish shooters expressed ideas that aroused concern about their violent intentions well before the shootings. Neither of them hid his sympathy for the previous school shootings. School friends of Auvinen had tried to convince him that the school shootings did not deserve admiration because of the loss of innocent lives.[28] Several days before the attack, Auvinen posted videos on YouTube featuring his newly purchased gun. In an Internet conversation, he commented on the gun policy in Finland: "Weird country, to give a gun to a maniac like me."[29]

Just one day before the shooting, his school friends had seen a picture of his gun on his Web page in IRC-Galleria and had enough concern to ask him whether he intended to commit a school shooting. He replied that he might commit a spree killing in the Finnish parliament because of the corrupt nature of politicians.[30]

The young people at the local youth club (situated near the school building) had expressed their concern about Auvinen's changed behavior. They were alarmed by remarks he made, such as yelling about a forthcoming white revolution and everyone being killed. A local youth worker discussed these matters with the school principal, but the principal did not think that Auvinen's behavior was alarming enough.[31] The principal was the final victim, executed in front of her school.

Saari disclosed his intentions on numerous occasions. In 2005, he had talked to his friend about going on a shooting spree in a restaurant in his former hometown. In 2006, he showed videos of American school shootings to a friend and said that he would like to do a similar massacre. In 2007, his friends observed his interest in the Columbine, Virginia Tech, and Jokela shootings. His former girlfriend claimed that Saari had been in Internet contact with Auvinen (although this contact was not verified by the Finnish police). In early 2008, Saari mentioned to his half-sister that he might commit a shooting at school.[32]

Friends and fellow students of Saari did not approve of his talk about school shootings. Some of them thought he was joking, but some were seriously concerned. During his exchange training in Hungary in 2008, his fellow Finnish students contacted school authorities both in Hungary and in Finland, because they were convinced that the situation would merit intervention. Peers had knowledge about Saari's leisure-time behavior, which included heavy use of alcohol. He made references to suicide and the Jokela shootings. He also seemed to be depressed and lonely. Saari's friends were extremely worried about his intentions to get a gun: "We often said that Matti should not get a gun." The same friend called Saari a couple of times to make sure that he would not do anything foolish with the gun.[33]

Kauhajoki police interviewed Saari a day before the shooting. The police inspector found no legal cause to arrest him or confiscate his gun.[34] This police officer was later charged with dereliction of duty, but was found not guilty.

Conclusions

The two Finnish school shooting cases are examples of failures in prevention. There are several avenues for prevention in these cases.[35] The first opportunity for early prevention takes place in childhood when many young boys are bullied. Anti-bullying programs might prove to be a method for preventing the escalation of abusive behavior that ultimately leads to violence. Schools should be better prepared to recognize and intervene when a student is a victim of chronic bullying.

A second opportunity for prevention occurs when a student develops symptoms of mental disorder. Students suffering from anxiety and depression, and who are ostracized from their peers, should be offered adequate mental health treatment. Even immediately before the acts, the symptoms of mental disorder in these boys were not recognized as serious concerns and the student health services in Finland were not adequately organized to be able to respond to their needs.

A third opportunity for prevention occurs when students express their thoughts of violence to their peers. In the Finnish cases, the immediate social peer groups did not encourage the school shootings and they stood as an opposing force, but unfortunately it was not powerful enough to prevent the shootings.

On-line communities offered a more sympathetic audience where these boys could talk about previous shootings and develop a violent identity. The Internet provided the school shooters with detailed information about shootings, access to friends who shared their interests and indirectly encouraged their plans, and finally, a means of realizing their fantasies of public fame through file-sharing Web sites where they could post personal manifestos. One can conclude from this that knowledge about the on-line identity and groups a student identifies with might be important when assessing a potential threat.

Peer groups off- and on-line had knowledge that adults did not have. The off-line peer group was aware of the shooter's interest in school shootings. These peers were worried and expressed their concerns to the would-be shooters and contacted school authorities, but the seriousness of the situation was not recognized. Other young people were aware of the acquired gun. Some of the remarks, photos, and videos could be classified as leakages in which a student expresses attitudes, intentions, or thoughts that could signal an impending violent act.[36]

To prevent school shootings it is vital to have both threat assessment procedures in place and relationships based on trust so that young people can be confident that their information will be handled in a fair and reliable way.

Notes

1. Sahlberg, P. (2010). Educational change in Finland. In A. Hargreaves, A. Lieberman, M. Fullan, & D. Hopkins (Eds.), *Second international handbook of educational change* (Part 1, pp. 323–348). New York: Springer.

2. Currie, C., Gabhainn, S. N., Godeau, E., Roberts, C., Smith, R., Currie, D., & Barnekow, V. (Eds.). (2008). *Inequalities in young people's health. HBSC international report from the 2005/2006 survey.* Copenhagen, Denmark: WHO Regional Office for Europe. P. 43.

3. Kämppi, K., Välimaa, R., Tynjälä, J., Haapasalo, I., Vilberg, J., & Kannas, L. (2008). *Peruskoulun 5. 7.ja 9.luokan oppilaiden koulukokemukset ja koettu terveys. WHO-koululaistutkimuksen trendejä vuosina 1994–2006* [School experiences and experienced health of the pupils from 5th, 7th and 9th grade. Trends of WHO pupil investigation in 1994–2006]. Jyväskylä, Finland: Finnish National Board of Education and University of Jyväskylä. Pp. 23–24.

4. Salmi, V. (2009). Nuorten rikoskäyttäytyminen 1995–2008 [Self-reported juvenile delinquency in Finland, 1995–2008]. In V. Salmi (Ed.), *Nuorten rikoskäyttäytyminen ja uhrikokemukset. Nuorisorikollisuuskyselyiden tuloksia 1995–2008* (Research Report No. 246, pp. 1–43). Helsinki, Finland: National Research Institute of Legal Policy.

5. National Health Survey. (2009). *School bullying.* Retrieved from http://info.stakes.fi/kouluterveyskysely/FI/tulokset/taulukot2009/kiusaaminen2009.htm.

6. Kääriäinen, J. (2008). Väkivalta rikoksena [Violence as a crime]. In N. Ellonen, J.Kääriäinen, V. Salmi, & H. Sariola (Eds.), *Lasten ja nuorten väkivaltakokemukset* [Violence experiences of children and the young] (pp. 41–51). Tampere and Helsinki, Finland: Police College of Finland and National Research Institute of Legal Policy.

7. Peura, J., Pelkonen, M., & Kirves, L. (2009). *Miksi kertoisin, kun se ei auta? Raportti nuorten kiusaamiskyselystä* [Why would I tell, because it does not help: A report on bullying survey for young people]. Helsinki, Finland: Mannerheim League for Child Welfare. Pp. 30–32.

8. National Bureau of Investigation. (1989). *Raumanmeren koulusurmien esitutkintapöytäkirja* [Pre-trial investigation report of the Raumanmeri school killings]. Rauma, Finland: National Bureau of Investigation. Pp. 25–26.

9. Investigation Commission of the Jokela School Shooting. (2009). *Jokela school shooting on 7 November 2007. Report of the Investigation Commission.* Helsinki, Finland: Ministry of Justice. Pp. 49, 51, 108.

10. Oksanen, A., Räsänen, P., Nurmi, J., & Lindström, K. (2010). "This can't happen here!" Community reactions to school shootings in Finland. *Research on Finnish Society, 3,* 19–27.

11. National Bureau of Investigation. (2009). *Kauhajoen koulusurmien esitutkintapöytäkirja* [Pre-trial investigation report of the Kauhajoki school killings]. Vaasa, Finland: National Bureau of Investigation. Pp. 39, 40, 67–69.

12. Investigation Commission of the Kauhajoki School Shooting. (2010). *Kauhajoen koulusurmat 23.9.2008* [Kauhajoki school shooting on 23 September 2008 Report of the Investigation Commission] (Reports 11/2010). Helsinki, Finland: Ministry of Justice. Pp. 55–59.

13. National Bureau of Investigation. (2009). P. 41.

14. Verlinden, S., Hersen, M., & Thomas, J. (2000). Risk factors in school shootings. *Clinical Psychology Review, 20,* 8–56. P. 13.

15. Harding, D. J., Fox, C., & Mehta, J. (2002). Studying rare events through qualitative case studies: Lessons from a study of rampage school shootings. *Sociological Methods & Research, 31,* 174–217; Kidd, S. T., & Meyer, C. L. (2005). Similarities of school shootings in rural and small communities. *Journal of Rural Community Psychology, E5*(1); Newman, K., Fox, C., Harding, D., Mehta, J., & Roth, W. (2004). *Rampage. The social roots of school shootings.* New York: Basic Books.

16. Nurmi, J., Räsänen, P., & Oksanen, A. (in press). The norm of solidarity: Experiencing negative aspects of community life after a school shooting tragedy. *Journal of Social Work*; see also Ryan, J., & Hawdon, J. (2008). From individual to community: The "framing" of 4–16 and the display of social solidarity. *Traumatology, 14,* 43–51.

17. Sourander, A., Jensen, P., Rönning, J. A., Niemelä, S., Helenius, H., Sillanmäki, L., & Almqvist, F. (2007). What is the early adulthood outcome of boys who bully or are bullied in childhood? The Finnish "From a Boy to a Man" study. *Pediatrics, 120,* 397–404.

18. Fekkes, M., Pijpers, F., Fredriks, A., Vogels, T., & Verloove-Vanhorick, S. (2006). Do bullied children get ill, or do ill children get bullied? A prospective cohort study on the relationship between bullying and health-related symptoms. *Pediatrics, 117,* 1568–1574.

19. Investigation Commission of the Jokela School Shooting. (2008). P. 51.

20. Investigation Commission of the Kauhajoki School Shooting. (2010). Pp. 56–58.

21. Myllyniemi, S. (2009). *Nuorisobarometri 2009* [The youth barometer 2009]. Helsinki: Finnish Youth Research Network, Ministry of Education and Culture and National Advisory Council for Youth Affairs. Pp. 88–92.

22. National Bureau of Investigation (2008). *Jokelan koulusurmien esitutkintapöytäkirja* [Pre-trial investigation report of the Jokela school killings]. Helsinki, Finland: National Bureau of Investigation. Pp. 403–405.

23. National Bureau of Investigation. (2008). Pp. 17–19.

24. National Bureau of Investigation. (2009). Pp. 51–52, 65–66.

25. Investigation Commission of the Kauhajoki School Shooting. (2010).

26. Semenov, A., Veijalainen, J., & Kyppö, J. (2010). Analyzing the presence of school-shooting related communities at social media sites. *International Journal of Multimedia Intelligence and Security, 1*(3), 232–268.

27. Fast, J. (2008). *Ceremonial violence. A psychological explanation of school shootings.* New York: Overlook. Pp. 193–194.

28. National Bureau of Investigation. (2008). P. 433.

29. National Bureau of Investigation. (2008). P. 19.

30. National Bureau of Investigation. (2008). P. 491.

31. Kiilakoski, T. (2009). *Viiltoja. Analyysi kouluväkivallasta Jokelassa.* [Cuts. An analysis of school violence in Jokela]. Helsinki, Finland: Finnish Youth Research Network. Retrieved from http://www.nuorisotutkimusseura.fi/julkaisuja/viiltoja.pdf. P. 53.

32. National Bureau of Investigation. (2009). Pp. 41–48, 72–74, 280–281.
33. National Bureau of Investigation. (2009). Pp. 302–303.
34. Investigation Commission of the Kauhajoki School Shooting. (2010). Pp. 52–54.
35. See Bondü, R., & Scheithauer, H. (2010). Explaining and preventing school shootings: Chances and difficulties of control. In W. Heitmeyer, H. G. Haupt, S. Malthaner, & A. Kirschner (Eds.), *Control of violence: Historical and international perspectives on violence in modern societies* (pp. 295–314). New York: Springer.
36. O'Toole, M. E. (2000). *The school shooter. A threat assessment perspective.* Quantico, VA: Federal Bureau of Investigation. Pp. 22–23; Bondü, R., & Scheithauer, H. (2009). School shootings in Deutschland: Aktuelle Trends zur Prävention vor schwerer, zielgericheter Gewalt an deutschen Schulen. *Praxis der Kinderpsychologie und Kinderpsychiatrie, 58,* 685–701.

TOMI KIILAKOSKI *is a researcher in the Finnish Youth Research Network. His research interests include school violence and its prevention, youth participation, and educational policy and philosophy.*

ATTE OKSANEN, *adjunct professor of social psychology, works as a researcher in the University of Tampere, Finland. He is leading the research project Everyday Life and Insecurity: Social Relations after the Jokela and Kauhajoki School Shootings (Aaltonen Foundation 2009–2012) with Professor Pekka Räsänen.*

As a problem-solving strategy to prevent violence, the Virginia Student Threat Assessment Guidelines permit school authorities to recognize and respond to the developmental complexities of children and adolescents without resorting to inflexible practices such as violence profiling or zero tolerance discipline.

3

A developmental perspective on the Virginia Student Threat Assessment Guidelines

Dewey G. Cornell

TWO MONTHS AFTER THE 1999 shootings at Columbine High School, the Federal Bureau of Investigation (FBI) convened a conference to determine whether it was possible to construct a behavioral profile of homicidal students that could be used to prevent school shootings. Both the FBI study[1] and a separate study by the U.S. Secret Service[2] found that many of the students felt rejected and victimized by their peers, mistreated by school authorities, and unloved by their parents. The students spent many hours preoccupied with entertainment violence through movies, music, or video games. Many of the youths could be described as narcissistic, paranoid, manipulative, alienated, and depressed. Despite an abundance of descriptive characteristics, both law enforcement agencies concluded that it was not possible to develop a useful profile or

NEW DIRECTIONS FOR YOUTH DEVELOPMENT, NO. 129, SPRING 2011 © WILEY PERIODICALS, INC.
Published online in Wiley Online Library (wileyonlinelibrary.com) • DOI: 10.1002/yd.386

checklist of a homicidal student, because such characteristics can be found in so many students who were not violent. There was no set of characteristics that had sufficient specificity to avoid a high false-positive rate.[3] As the FBI concluded,

One response to the pressure for action may be an effort to identify the next shooter by developing a "profile" of the typical school shooter. This may sound like a reasonable preventive measure, but in practice, trying to draw up a catalogue or "checklist" of warning signs to detect a potential shooter can be shortsighted, even dangerous. Such lists, publicized by the media, can end up unfairly labeling many nonviolent students as potentially dangerous or even lethal. In fact, a great many adolescents who will never commit violent acts will show some of the behaviors or personality traits included on the list.[1]

The FBI's conclusions contradicted many authorities who had disseminated checklists of warning signs for identifying a homicidal student. These warning signs were essentially unvalidated profiles that included broad characteristics found in many nonviolent youth. For example, the sixteen warning signs in the U.S. government's guide[4] included such items as history of discipline problems, drug use and alcohol use, feelings of being picked on and persecuted, and excessive feelings of rejection. These signs are better regarded as real problems (for example, substance abuse) that merit attention in their own right, rather than as predictors of homicidal violence. Another example is the American Psychological Association's "warning signs" pamphlet.[5] This document ominously states, "If you see these immediate warning signs, violence is a serious possibility." The list of immediate warning signs includes "increase in risk-taking behavior," "increase in use of drugs or alcohol," "significant vandalism or property damage," and "loss of temper on a daily basis." Most school authorities could identify students in their schools who meet these signs, yet fail to pose a serious threat for violence.

As the authors of the U.S. government's warning-signs report cautioned, "Unfortunately, *there is a real danger that early warning signs will be misinterpreted*."[4] They urged school authorities to

NEW DIRECTIONS FOR YOUTH DEVELOPMENT • DOI: 10.1002/yd

refrain from using the warning signs as a basis for punishing students or excluding them from school and they expressed concern that the warning signs could be used without regard to the student's situational or developmental context.

A more promising strategy for preventing homicidal acts of violence can be found in the findings by both the FBI[1] and Secret Service[2] that most of the attackers communicated or leaked their intentions to others prior to their attack. Many of the students had spent weeks or months contemplating, planning, and preparing to attack, and had often confided their ideas to friends or classmates. In some instances they sought assistance in obtaining a weapon or carrying out an attack, and in other cases they issued warnings to persons they did not want to harm or expressed anger toward those they wanted to kill. All of these behaviors reflected the strong developmental need of adolescents for peer acknowledgment. Similarly, the decision to carry out an attack in the open, public setting of a school reflected the adolescent's need to make a compelling statement to an audience of peers.

The adolescent's need to make his or her intentions known to others raised the possibility that shootings could be prevented by investigating student threats or related behavior suggesting plans or preparations for an attack. This investigative process has been labeled *threat assessment.*[1,6] Student threat assessment can be distinguished from profiling in part because the investigation is triggered by the student's own threatening behavior rather than by some broader combination of student characteristics.[7] Moreover, threat assessment does not attempt to match a suspect to a profile, but to investigate whether the person has engaged in behavior suggesting he or she is engaged in a pattern of behavior leading toward a violent act.[1,6] Any student can make a threat, but relatively few have a persisting violent intent that leads them to engage in the planning and preparation necessary to carry out an attack.

Although a student's threat might be a useful indicator of an impending attack, it is not a necessary or sufficient condition for violence. Some attacks do occur without prior threats, and many threats do not lead to violence. For example, in a self-report survey

NEW DIRECTIONS FOR YOUTH DEVELOPMENT • DOI: 10.1002/yd

of nearly 10,000 students, Singer and Flannery[8] found that more than half of secondary school boys and more than one-third of primary school boys reported threatening to hurt someone in the past year. Students who made threats had an increased likelihood of also reporting a physical assault, including assault with a knife or gun, but threats were not uniformly associated with violent outcomes.

High-profile acts of violence can produce outbreaks of copycat threats. Kotinsky, Bixler, and Kettl[9] reported 354 threats of school violence in the state of Pennsylvania alone during the 50 days after the 1999 Columbine shootings. Although none of these threats resulted in bombings, shootings, or other threatened acts, they were often disruptive to the school and a source of anxiety to the community. These findings make it clear that threats are only a starting point for careful assessment of a student's potential for violence.

As the FBI noted in their report, "all threats are not created equal."[1] Compared to adults, students are immature, developing individuals whose emotions and passions can more easily override their reasoning skills and judgment. Children, and to a lesser extent, adolescents, are more prone to express themselves impulsively and irrationally than are adults. They are also less careful and observant of their actions and more likely to make mistakes that violate school rules and policies. This means that their statements and actions cannot be taken literally and must be evaluated within a situational context and from a developmental perspective. A zero tolerance policy that does not consider the context and meaning of the student's behavior is developmentally inappropriate and has resulted in numerous cases in which schools have overreacted.[10,11] For example, students in the United States have been removed from school for misbehavior such as bringing a one-inch plastic toy gun to school, bringing a plastic knife to school for use at lunchtime, pointing a finger like a gun and playfully pretending to shoot someone, and making threatening statements in jest. There is no evidence that such policies and practices have any beneficial impact on students or improve school safety.[10]

Student misbehavior must be assessed for its meaning and intent. As the Secret Service recommended in its report, once a student has been identified as *making* a threat, an evaluation is needed to determine whether the student *poses* a threat.[2] If the threat is confirmed as serious, the next step is to take action to prevent the threat from being carried out.

The Secret Service and U.S. Department of Education placed the concept of threat assessment in a broader context of creating a safe school climate and recommended accompanying efforts such as addressing bullying and resolving student conflicts, fostering trust and communication between students and adults, and encouraging students to break the code of silence and seek help for threats of violence.[12] The Virginia model for threat assessment incorporates this perspective and uses each case of a student threat as an opportunity for preventive action. From this perspective, threat assessment might be more properly regarded as threat management. The FBI concluded its report by citing "a compelling need to field test, evaluate and further develop these threat assessment recommendations and to develop appropriate interventions designed to respond to the mental health needs of the students involved."[1]

The Virginia Student Threat Assessment Model

In response to the FBI and Secret Service reports, researchers at the University of Virginia developed a set of guidelines for school administrators to use in responding to a student threat of violence.[11,13] The guidelines steer school authorities through a decision-tree process of investigation accompanied by efforts to resolve the conflict or problem that led the student to make a threat (see Figure 3.1). After a preliminary assessment of the reported threat, school administrators determine whether the case can be easily resolved as a transient threat (such as a remark made in jest or in a brief state of anger) or will require more extensive assessment and protective action as a substantive threat. In the most serious cases,

Figure 3.1. Decision tree for student threat assessment

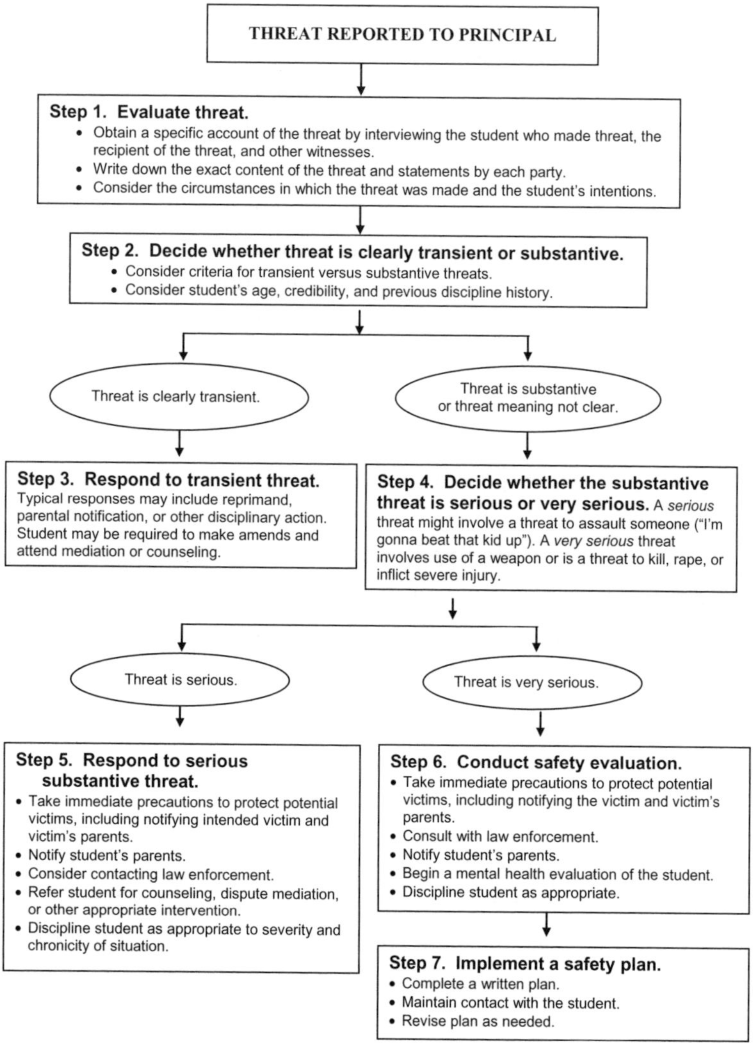

THREAT REPORTED TO PRINCIPAL

Step 1. Evaluate threat.
- Obtain a specific account of the threat by interviewing the student who made threat, the recipient of the threat, and other witnesses.
- Write down the exact content of the threat and statements by each party.
- Consider the circumstances in which the threat was made and the student's intentions.

Step 2. Decide whether threat is clearly transient or substantive.
- Consider criteria for transient versus substantive threats.
- Consider student's age, credibility, and previous discipline history.

Threat is clearly transient.

Threat is substantive or threat meaning not clear.

Step 3. Respond to transient threat. Typical responses may include reprimand, parental notification, or other disciplinary action. Student may be required to make amends and attend mediation or counseling.

Step 4. Decide whether the substantive threat is serious or very serious. A *serious* threat might involve a threat to assault someone ("I'm gonna beat that kid up"). A *very serious* threat involves use of a weapon or is a threat to kill, rape, or inflict severe injury.

Threat is serious.

Threat is very serious.

Step 5. Respond to serious substantive threat.
- Take immediate precautions to protect potential victims, including notifying intended victim and victim's parents.
- Notify student's parents.
- Consider contacting law enforcement.
- Refer student for counseling, dispute mediation, or other appropriate intervention.
- Discipline student as appropriate to severity and chronicity of situation.

Step 6. Conduct safety evaluation.
- Take immediate precautions to protect potential victims, including notifying the victim and victim's parents.
- Consult with law enforcement.
- Notify student's parents.
- Begin a mental health evaluation of the student.
- Discipline student as appropriate.

Step 7. Implement a safety plan.
- Complete a written plan.
- Maintain contact with the student.
- Revise plan as needed.

a multidisciplinary team will conduct a comprehensive safety evaluation that would include both a law enforcement investigation and a mental health assessment of the student.

Team composition

Each school should have its own threat assessment team, consisting of an administrator (principal or assistant principal), a law

NEW DIRECTIONS FOR YOUTH DEVELOPMENT • DOI: 10.1002/yd

enforcement representative (such as a school resource officer), and one or more mental health professionals (school psychologist, counselor, social worker, etc.). A local school-based team is recommended for several reasons. First, in the case of a serious threat, there must be an immediate response; if a student threatens to kill someone, school administrators cannot wait for a team of outside experts to be assembled. Second, threat assessment requires a careful consideration of contextual and situational factors. A school-based team is more familiar with the school environment, recent events at the school, and the students involved in the threat. Finally, most student threats are not serious enough to warrant summoning an external team. When a student makes a rash or angry statement that can be easily resolved, use of an outside team would be inefficient and also run the risk of magnifying the importance of such events. Of course, local teams can call upon external consultants in unusual cases where additional expertise is needed.

School principals or assistant principals should lead the threat assessment team because they are responsible for student discipline and safety. Because student threats are usually treated as disciplinary violations, the student can readily be referred to the administrator for both disciplinary and threat assessment purposes. As team leader, the principal conducts a triage evaluation to determine the seriousness of the threat. In the simplest situations, the principal takes the limited action necessary to resolve the incident, and if the threat is more complex, involves the full team. In all cases, the principal leads the team and makes final decisions about how to respond to the threat.

Teams should include a law enforcement representative, ideally, a school resource officer who has been trained to work in schools. The school resource officer advises the team whether a student's behavior has violated the law and can instruct students and staff on law enforcement matters. Perhaps most importantly, school resource officers can be a role model and encourage law-abiding behavior by interacting with students and participating in school functions. School resource officers can have a positive effect on the school climate by maintaining positive, friendly relations with students and monitoring potentially volatile conflicts between students or groups of students. In the most serious cases, the officer responds to emergencies or crises, such as when there is an imminent risk of violence. In these cases, the officer has the same law enforcement duties and authority that he or she would have when an incident takes place outside of school, such as arresting a person wielding a weapon or obtaining a search warrant for a student's home.

In the most serious cases, the school psychologist conducts a mental health evaluation of the student with two main objectives. The first objective is to screen the student for mental health problems that demand immediate attention, such as psychosis or suicidality. The second objective is to assess why the student made the threat and make recommendations for dealing with the problem or conflict that stimulated the threatening behavior.

Overall, the school psychologist follows a *risk-reduction* or *risk-management* approach, as distinguished from a predictive approach.[14] Although it is understandable for school authorities to want a formal prediction whether a student will carry out a threat, such predictions tend to be unreliable and prone to error.[15] The prediction of violence is complex and communications about violence risk are easily misstated or misinterpreted.[16] Even though psychologists can make reasonably accurate short-term predictions of violence in some situations,[16] little is known about the prediction of student violence.[15] For these reasons, the Virginia Guidelines discourage school psychologists from trying to predict whether a student will carry out the threatened action.

Furthermore, any substantial risk of violence requires that school authorities take protective action. A formal risk assessment estimating that the risk is 20%, 50%, or 90% is not especially useful and may be subject to misinterpretation. Since risk is a dynamic process that can change in response to events in the student's daily life, static estimates of risk are potentially misleading. The goal of threat assessment is always to reduce risk through interventions aimed at the problems that led to the threat.

The school counselor and other mental health professionals bring expertise in working with troubled students and helping them resolve personal problems and conflicts in their relationships. Schools in the United States have varying staffing patterns and may include social workers, student assistance professionals, substance abuse counselors, and other mental health professionals. These team members might identify resources that could serve the student or take a direct role in providing services to the student, such as individual counseling for anger management or social skills training to improve peer relationships. He or she can serve as the team member who monitors the student's participation in the intervention plan and assesses its impact and continued effectiveness.

Threat assessment process

Threat assessment teams follow a seven-step decision tree that is explained in a manual with an extensive set of guidelines and case examples.[13] At step one, the leader of the threat assessment team interviews the student who made the threat. The interviewer uses a standard set of questions that can be adapted to the specific situation. The principal should also interview witnesses to the threat and make notes on a standard form. The principal is not concerned simply with the verbal content of the threat, but the context in which the threat was made and what the student meant and intended in making the threat.

At step two, the principal must make an important distinction between threats that are serious, in the sense that they pose a continuing risk or danger to others, and those that are not serious, because they are readily resolved and do not pose a continuing risk. Less serious threats that are readily resolved, termed *transient* threats, are distinguished from *substantive* threats. Transient threats are defined as behaviors that can be readily identified as expressions of anger or frustration—or perhaps inappropriate attempts at humor—but which dissipate quickly when the student has time to reflect on the meaning of what he or she has said. The most important feature of a transient threat is that the student does not have a sustained intention to harm someone.

Transient threats, which are the most common form of threats, are resolved at step three when the principal (or other team members) is able to resolve the threat fairly easily without conducting a comprehensive threat assessment. The student should be willing to apologize or explain to those affected by threat, or take other action to make amends for his or her behavior. A transient threat may have been sparked by an argument or conflict, and in such cases the principal may involve other team members in helping to resolve the problem. The principal may respond with a reprimand or other disciplinary consequence, but is not compelled to take protective action because the threat is not a serious threat. Substantive threats represent a sustained intent to harm someone beyond the immediate incident or argument during which the threat was made.

If there is doubt whether a threat is transient or substantive, the threat is treated as substantive. Substantive threats may be identified by several features that are regarded as *presumptive, but not necessary or sufficient,* indicators. The presumptive indicators, derived from the FBI report,[1] include:

- the threat includes plausible details, such as a specific victim, time, place, and method of assault;
- the threat has been repeated over time or communicated to multiple persons;
- the threat is reported as a plan, or planning has taken place;
- the student has accomplices, or has attempted to recruit accomplices;
- the student has invited an audience of peers to watch the threatened event;
- there is physical evidence of intent to carry out the threat, such as a weapon, bomb materials, map, or written plan.

Although the presence of any one of these features may lead the school administrator to presume the threat is substantive, none are absolute indicators; with additional investigation, other facts could demonstrate that the threat is transient. For example, a student might ask an accomplice to deliver a threatening letter to a classmate. The threat is transient if the student does not intend to carry out the threat, but only means to frighten the classmate. Such an incident would be handled as a serious disciplinary matter, but not as a serious threat.

The example of a student who frightens a classmate with a transient threat illustrates another important point, which is that threat assessment and discipline are separate processes. In some cases, the disciplinary consequences can be quite severe even if the threat is transient. For example, a false bomb threat is not substantive if the student only intends to disrupt the school, but it still has serious legal consequences. In general, threat assessment is concerned with the risk of future harm to others and what steps should be taken to prevent the threat from being carried out, whereas discipline is concerned with punishing a student as a consequence for his or her actions.

In essence, threat assessment teams must always consider the context of the threat and make reasoned judgments based on all the available information. The team should consider the student's age and capabilities, mental stability, prior history of violent behavior, and other relevant factors. The guidelines assist the team in its investigation, but do not provide a prescription or formula.

If the threat is determined to be a substantive threat, the principal proceeds to step four and distinguishes whether the substantive threat is *serious* or *very serious*, a distinction based on the intended severity of injury. A *serious* threat is a threat to assault, strike, or beat up someone. A *very serious* threat is a threat to kill, sexually assault, or severely injure someone. A threat involving the use of a weapon is generally considered a threat to severely injure someone. However, teams must always use their judgment. For example, if a student threatens to shoot someone with a rubber band, this is technically a weapon, but it would not make sense to treat such a threat as very serious.

In the case of a serious substantive threat, the team moves to step five. At step five, school authorities are obliged to act to protect potential victims. These protective actions depend on the circumstances of the threat, as well as any information indicating how soon and where the threat might be carried out. Immediate protective actions include cautioning the student about the consequences of carrying out the threat and providing supervision so that the student cannot carry out the threat while at school. A team member should contact the student's parents, so that the parents can assume responsibility for supervising the student after school.

Very serious threats require the most extensive action by the team. At step six, the team takes immediate protective actions in response to the threat, and at step seven the team completes a thorough evaluation of the student (termed a "safety evaluation"), which leads to implementation of a long-term "safety plan." In very serious substantive cases, the law enforcement officer on the team must determine whether the student has violated the law, and if so, what law enforcement action should be taken. The team must notify the intended victim, and if the victim is a student, the victim's parents. The school psychologist should begin a mental health evaluation of the student as soon as possible, with the initial goal of assessing the student's mental state and need for immediate mental health services. The student should be suspended from school pending a complete assessment of the threat and determination of the most appropriate school placement.

At step seven, the team completes a safety evaluation that integrates findings from all available sources of information in a written safety plan. The safety plan is designed both to protect potential victims and to address the student's educational needs. The plan may include mental health and counseling recommendations, findings from the law enforcement investigation, and disciplinary consequences. At this point, the principal decides whether the student can return to school or should be placed in an alternative setting.

Threat assessment research findings

The first field test of the threat assessment guidelines was conducted in thirty-five schools spanning grades K–12.[17] The Virginia researchers trained a team in each school that followed the threat assessment guidelines for each case of a student threat that was reported by someone (teacher, student, parent, or others) to school authorities. Across 188 cases collected over one school year, most (70 percent) were resolved as transient threats through an explanation or apology, although often with some disciplinary consequences and counseling. The remaining 30 percent were substantive threats that required protective action and the development of a plan to address the underlying conflict or problem that drove the student to make a threat. Only three students (each with a lengthy record of disciplinary violations) were given long-term suspensions. Approximately half of the students received short-term suspensions (typically one to three days), and nearly all students were able to return to their original school. The following year, researchers conducted follow-up interviews with school principals and found that none of the threats were carried out.

A secondary analysis[18] compared outcomes for students receiving special education services with students in regular education programs (using the original sample plus sixty-eight additional cases). This study demonstrated that threat assessment could be used with students in special education programs and that the students in regular and special education received comparable disciplinary and behavioral outcomes.

A second field test[19] was conducted in Memphis City Schools, a large urban school system serving a predominantly (87 percent) African-American population. Approximately 75 percent of Memphis students were eligible for free or reduced lunch and 29 percent of students had been retained at least one grade. Memphis was not prepared to train teams in each of its 194 schools, and already had an established center that consulted with its schools, so the assessment approach was adapted for use within this system. A single centralized team provided evaluations for cases referred from any school in the division. One consequence of this decision is that assessments were conducted only on students whose behavior was judged serious enough by the school principal to merit a suspension of four or more days.

The Memphis evaluation examined 209 cases that represented the most serious disciplinary violations committed by students in 103 schools. There were sixty (29 percent) threats to hit or beat up someone, forty-eight (23 percent) threats to cut or stab, thirty-two (15 percent) threats to shoot, thirty (14 percent) threats to kill, fourteen (7 percent) sexual threats, and twenty-five (12 percent) other threats (such as to blow up or burn down the school). In each case, the centralized team developed an individualized plan of mental health and educational services. All but five students were able to return to school or an alternative educational placement, and just three students were incarcerated. Across all sources of information, there was no report of any of the threats being carried out. In addition, the study examined student discipline referrals before and after the threat assessment for 198 students with available records. These students averaged 6.4 referrals before the threat incident and 2.9 referrals after the threat assessment, a statistically significant decline of 55 percent.

The two field test studies found that schools could carry out a threat assessment approach with seemingly positive outcomes, but both are limited by the absence of comparison groups. A third study[20] addressed this limitation in a statewide survey of Virginia public high schools. According to the state's annual school safety audit, by 2007 ninety-five (34 percent) high schools had adopted the Virginia threat assessment guidelines, 131 (47 percent) schools used locally developed threat assessment procedures, and 54 (19 percent) reported not using a threat assessment approach. The three groups were compared retrospectively with the use of a school climate survey that had been administered to randomly selected samples of ninth-grade students in each high school as part of the Virginia High School Safety Study.[21]

Students in schools using the Virginia threat assessment guidelines reported less bullying in the past thirty days, greater willingness to seek help for bullying and threats of violence, and more positive perceptions of the school climate than students in either of the other two groups of schools.[20] In addition, schools using the Virginia guidelines had fewer long-term suspensions during the 2006–2007 school year than schools using other threat assessment approaches. Group differences could not be attributed to school size, minority composition, socioeconomic status of the student body, neighborhood violent crime, or the extent of security measures in the schools, which were statistically controlled.

A fifth study examined the effects of threat assessment training on school staff.[22] School teams typically are trained in a six-hour workshop to follow threat assessment guidelines described in a 145-page manual.[13] A key goal of the training model is to convince school staff members to use a threat assessment approach rather than a zero tolerance approach. School administrators are keenly concerned about the potential for a serious act of violence, and many make use of zero tolerance policies, typically involving long-term suspension. Threat assessment and zero tolerance are essentially antithetical approaches, because the former considers the context and meaning of the student's behavior, and calibrates the response to the seriousness of the threat, whereas the latter imposes a uniform sanction regardless of the circumstances.

In the training study, Allen, Cornell, and Lorek[22] administered pre- and post-workshop surveys to 351 multidisciplinary staff from two school divisions, one serving a challenging urban population and the other a more affluent, suburban population. Comparison of pre- and post-measures showed that there was a substantial decrease among school staff members in support for zero tolerance and increased knowledge of threat assessment principles and concepts. These changes were found among staff in both school divisions, with similar effects across school principals, psychologists, counselors, resource officers, and social workers.

Together, the findings from these five published studies provide promising support for the use of the Virginia Student Threat Assessment Guidelines, but more research is needed. There is a need to conduct a randomized controlled study of schools using threat assessment versus alternative approaches, to examine changes in schools before and after implementation of threat assessment, to determine standards for fidelity and compliance with the guidelines, and to investigate the impact on individual students—aggressors and victims—who participate in the intervention. Work in these areas is under way.

Notes

1. O'Toole, M. E. (2000). *The school shooter: A threat assessment perspective.* Quantico, VA: National Center for the Analysis of Violent Crime, Federal Bureau of Investigation.

2. Vossekuil, B., Fein, R. A., Reddy, M., Borum, R., & Modzeleski, W. (2002). *The final report and findings of the Safe School Initiative: Implications for the prevention of school attacks in the United States.* Washington, DC: U.S. Secret Service and U.S. Department of Education.

3. Sewell, K. W., & Mendelsohn, M. (2000). Profiling potentially violent youth: Statistical and conceptual problems. *Children's Services: Social Policy, Research, and Practice, 3,* 147–169.

4. Dwyer, K., Osher, D., & Warger, C. (1998). *Early warning, timely response: A guide to safe schools.* Washington, DC: U.S. Department of Education.

5. American Psychological Association. (1999). *Warning signs.* Washington, DC: Author.

6. Randazzo, M. R., Borum, R., Vossekuil, B., Fein, R., Modzeleski, W., & Pollack, W. (2006). Threat assessment in schools: Empirical support and comparison with other approaches. In S. R. Jimerson & M. J. Furlong (Eds.), *The handbook of school violence and school safety: From research to practice* (pp. 147–156). Mahwah, NJ: Lawrence Erlbaum.

7. Reddy, M., Borum, R., Berglund, J.,Vossekuil, B. Fein, R., & Modzeleski, W. (2001). Evaluating risk for targeted violence in schools: Comparing risk assessment, threat assessment, and other approaches. *Psychology in the Schools, 38,* 157–172.

8. Singer, M., & Flannery, D. (2000). The relationship between children's threats of violence and violent behaviors. *Archives of Pediatric and Adolescent Medicine, 154,* 785–790.

9. Kotinsky, S., Bixler, E., & Kettl, P. (2001). Threats of school violence in Pennsylvania after media coverage of the Columbine High School massacre. *Archives of Pediatric and Adolescent Medicine, 155,* 994–1001.

10. American Psychological Association Zero Tolerance Task Force. (2008). Are zero tolerance policies effective in schools? An evidentiary review and recommendations. *American Psychologist, 63,* 852–862.

11. Cornell, D. (2006). *School violence: Fears versus facts.* Mahwah, NJ: Lawrence Erlbaum.

12. Fein, R., Vossekuil, B., Pollack, W., Borum, R., Modzeleski, W., & Reddy, M. (2002). *Threat assessment in schools: A guide to managing threatening*

situations and to creating safe school climates. Washington, DC: U.S. Secret Service and Department of Education.

13. Cornell, D., & Sheras, P. (2006). *Guidelines for responding to student threats of violence.* Longmont, CO: Sopris West.

14. Heilbrun, K. (1997). Prediction versus management models relevant to risk assessment: The importance of legal decision-making context. *Law and Human Behavior, 21,* 347–360.

15. Mulvey, E. P., & Cauffman, E. (2001). The inherent limits of predicting school violence. *American Psychologist, 56,* 797–802.

16. Borum, R. (1996). Improving the clinical practice of violence risk assessment: Technologies, guidelines and training. *American Psychologist, 51,* 945–956.

17. Cornell, D., Sheras, P., Kaplan, S., McConville, D., Douglass, J., Elkon, A., et al. (2004). Guidelines for student threat assessment: Field-test findings. *School Psychology Review, 33,* 527–546.

18. Kaplan, S., & Cornell, D. (2005). Threats of violence by students in special education. *Behavioral Disorders, 31,* 107–119.

19. Strong, K., & Cornell, D. (2008). Student threat assessment in Memphis City Schools: A descriptive report. *Behavioral Disorders, 34,* 42–54.

20. Cornell, D., Sheras, P., Gregory, A., & Fan, X. (2009). A retrospective study of school safety conditions in high schools using the Virginia Threat Assessment Guidelines versus alternative approaches. *School Psychology Quarterly, 24,* 119–129.

21. Gregory, A., Cornell, D., Fan, X., Sheras, P., & Shih, T. (2010). Authoritative school discipline: High school practices associated with lower student bullying and victimization. *Journal of Educational Psychology, 102,* 483–496.

22. Allen, K., Cornell, D., & Lorek, E. (2008). Response of school personnel to student threat assessment training. *School Effectiveness and School Improvement, 19,* 319–332.

DEWEY G. CORNELL *is professor of education, a forensic clinical psychologist, and director of the Virginia Youth Violence Project. He teaches in the Programs in Clinical and School Psychology in the Curry School of Education at the University of Virginia.*

Two projects have been designed to fill the gap between universal prevention and emergency response in preventing severe school violence in Germany.

4

Prevention of homicidal violence in schools in Germany: The Berlin Leaking Project and the Networks Against School Shootings Project (NETWASS)

*Vincenz Leuschner, Rebecca Bondü,
Miriam Schroer-Hippel, Jennifer Panno,
Katharina Neumetzler, Sarah Fisch,
Johanna Scholl, Herbert Scheithauer*

IN THE PAST DECADE, Germany has experienced more cases of homicidal violence targeting schools than any nation other than the United States. Twelve incidents have resulted in the deaths of twenty teachers and sixteen students. In response to these tragedies, many German schools have implemented two main types of

The NETWASS Project is funded by the Federal Ministry of Education and Research (BMBF), Germany.

NEW DIRECTIONS FOR YOUTH DEVELOPMENT, NO. 129, SPRING 2011 © WILEY PERIODICALS, INC.
Published online in Wiley Online Library (wileyonlinelibrary.com) • DOI: 10.1002/yd.387

prevention efforts: (1) universal measures, such as bullying prevention, and (2) emergency response plans. Although both approaches
are important, there is a large gap between programs for all students and plans for responding to a serious incident. Our goal was
to develop an indicated prevention program that provides help to
students who are experiencing problems that make them at risk for
violence. This article describes two sequential German projects,
the Berlin Leaking Project and the Networks Against School
Shootings Project (NETWASS).

The need for prevention in Germany

Homicidal school violence became a national concern in Germany
especially after tragic school shootings were carried out by former
students in Erfurt in 2001 and in Winnenden in 2009. These high-
profile school attacks had a traumatic impact on German society,
generating a great deal of anxiety and uncertainty among parents,
teachers, politicians, and journalists. Table 4.1 summarizes the
most serious cases.

These attacks exhibit considerable diversity in planning, choice
of weapon, and targeted victims. Following Fein et al.,[1] Vossekuil
et al.,[2] and Bondü and Scheithauer,[3] we use the definition of
"severe targeted school violence" as a subtype of homicidal violence at schools that involves targeted attacks by students or former students on specific persons within schools or on the school
institution as a whole. This definition excludes ordinary violent
acts such as bullying or fights at school, but encompasses all types
of lethal weapons, and also knives, axes, incendiary material, or
explosive charges.

The school shootings in Erfurt and Winnenden claimed high
numbers of casualties (fifteen and sixteen, respectively), before the
offenders committed suicide. As Table 4.1 shows, five of the twelve
offenders in Germany were former students who were expelled
from school before they committed a school shooting. The perpetrator in Brannenburg, for example, had to leave his vocational

NEW DIRECTIONS FOR YOUTH DEVELOPMENT • DOI: 10.1002/yd

Table 4.1. Cases of severe targeted school violence in Germany

Date, Location	Incident
November 9, 1999, Meissen, Saxonia	Student stabs one teacher to death with two knives.
March 16, 2000, Brannenburg, Bavaria	Student shoots his principal and tries to kill himself.
February 19, 2002, Freising, Bavaria	Former student shoots his principal, hurts a teacher, and then shoots himself.
April 26, 2002, Erfurt, Thuringia	Former student kills thirteen school staff members, two students, a police officer, and himself.
August 29, 2002, Behrenhoff, Mecklenburg-Western Pomerania	Student intends to kill his teacher with a knife, but is stopped at the beginning of his attack.
July 2, 2003, Coburg, Bavaria	Student shoots two teachers and kills himself.
November 20, 2006, Emsdetten, Northrhine-Westfalia	Former student wounds more than thirty people and then shoots himself.
July 23, 2008, Biberach, Baden-Wurttemberg	Student wounds the principal with a knife.
March 11, 2009, Winnenden, Baden-Wurttemberg	Former student shoots fifteen people to death and wounds eleven before he kills himself.
May 11, 2009, Sankt Augustin, Northrhine-Westfalia	Student tries to burn the school building.
September 17, 2009, Ansbach, Bavaria	Student wounds nine students and a teacher with an axe.
February 18, 2010, Ludwigshafen, Rhineland-Palatinate	Former student stabs his teacher to death and fires a blank gun several times.

school the day before he shot school members and himself. The offender in Erfurt had been expelled from secondary school half a year before the attack because he had falsified a medical certification that he was too sick to attend school. Both of the offenders from Emsdetten and Winnenden were former students who had graduated from their schools. Except for one case in Sankt Augustin involving a sixteen-year-old female perpetrator, all shootings were committed by male students. The cases of school shootings in the United States and Germany differ especially with regard to the higher casualty rate for teachers than students and the use of firearms. In Germany, the offenders often used weapons other than firearms, like knives or axes.

Beyond these cases, schools are confronted with high numbers of threats. For example, within three months of the Winnenden 2009 shooting, more than 100 threats of targeted school violence were registered in Berlin.[4] As a result, many parents are deeply concerned about the safety of their children and school authorities face difficulties in deciding what to do about threats. Thus, there is a clear need to develop and implement evidence-based preventive approaches in order to protect students and school staff from further offenses and to support school staff in dealing with a shattered sense of safety in students, parents, and teachers.

Political and legal responses following school shootings in Germany

The sixteen federal states of Germany responded to the school shootings by developing different kinds of prevention and intervention strategies. Each state has its own Ministry of Education, Ministry of the Interior, and specific laws and regulations. Thus, there are differences in education guidelines, teacher education and employment, and school administration, as well as differences in law enforcement practices that must be considered in developing nationwide prevention measures.

After both the Erfurt and Winnenden school shootings, there were expert meetings to develop prevention and emergency-response measures that included police officers, psychologists, and legal experts. An expert meeting after the Winnenden school shooting, for example, formulated eighty-three propositions with regard to prevention, early detection, and handling of school shootings.[5] Most expert proposals recommended a combination of crisis-response plans to reduce the negative impact of a violent attack and universal prevention measures, such as efforts to strengthen social competence in young children.

NEW DIRECTIONS FOR YOUTH DEVELOPMENT • DOI: 10.1002/yd

All German federal states established emergency guidelines for school principals on how to respond to crisis situations. They included binding agreements on how to act in emergency situations and how to handle explicit threats of school shootings and homicide. They included directions on how to evacuate the school building, how to cooperate with police and the media, and how to inform school personnel and parents. Most of these guidelines also recommended or required the installation of school internal "Krisenteams" (crisis intervention teams). State emergency guidelines have not yet been fully evaluated, although a few aspects of these guidelines were examined in the Berlin Leaking Project (see below).

Many schools also made improvements to building security, such as adding special locks to classroom doors, establishing announcements for emergency situations, installing alarm buttons in every classroom, and placing signs to mark escape routes. Police departments trained special forces for emergency response and evacuation procedures, too. As with the emergency guidelines, evaluations of these security measures have not been conducted. Such evaluations should also check for unintended outcomes among students or staff members, such as increased anxiety or perceived vulnerability of schools.

One legislative reaction was the modification of the German gun control law in 2003 and 2009.[6] The 2003 law increased the standards for obtaining a weapons possession card and tightened the guideline for weapons storage. The law also expanded the list of banned objects to include many different knives and throwing stars. Furthermore, objects that look like a weapon or a forbidden object were banned as well. The 2009 law permitted more aggressive investigation of compliance with gun-possession requirements. Although Germany's strict weapon control laws may help prevent violence by limiting access to lethal weapons, there is acknowledgment among experts that weapon control alone cannot fully prevent school shootings.

The expert meetings all endorsed the use of universal school violence prevention programs and programs to promote a positive school or class climate, some of which already existed in German schools.[7] There were only a few recommendations for indicated prevention programs[8] although there was some support for the threat assessment approach advised by the U.S. Secret Service[9] and developed for U.S. schools.[10] Evaluation studies revealed that universal prevention programs can meet their immediate objectives[11] and will reduce risk factors associated with homicidal violence, but it would be most difficult to determine whether they can prevent school shootings.

Evaluation of responses to severe targeted school violence

Generally speaking, it is difficult to evaluate prevention efforts because the nonoccurrence of an incident, such as a school shooting, cannot be identified and attributed to the intervention measure. Because of the low base rate of school shootings[12] and the nonspecificity of known risk factors,[13] most German experts hold that such acts cannot be predicted in the long run.[14] Lists of risk factors and warning signs result from a few retrospective case studies, are not specific, and include features that might be correlates but not necessary or sufficient as causal factors.[15] Thus, profiling based on these putative warning signs could result in false-positive predictions, associated with stigmatization and hypersensitivity, which may raise more problems then it solves.[16] Indicated prevention programs must take into account various conditions such as the school climate,[17] information transfer in and between schools and other public institutions,[18] as well as accountability and attentiveness of professionals.

Studies from the United States indicate that certain models of threat assessment implemented in the school context may be useful and effective. Student threat assessment, like the Virginia model,[19] can be distinguished from profiling in part because the investigation is triggered by some form of student threat behavior rather than some unspecific risk profiles, warning signs, or a combination of demographic and personal characteristics of the student. Evaluation studies of this approach[20] found that none of the student threats treated according to the threat assessment model was carried out, although it was not possible to conclude that the threat assessment program caused this outcome. Nevertheless, planned severe acts of violence in schools basically seem to be identifiable, thanks to observable behaviors prior to the offense.[21]

The Berlin Leaking Project

The main aim of the Berlin Leaking Project was to investigate whether leaking by students can be a starting point for the prevention of school shootings. The concept of "leaking" was introduced by the U.S. Federal Bureau of Investigation as a potential means of identifying students planning to carry out a school shooting.[22] Generally, leaking refers to any communication of one's secret intentions. With reference to homicidal violence, leaking can include communications of violent fantasies and the planning of violent attacks, as well as conspicuous behavior that may be exhibited in planning to carry out an attack.[23] Because leaking concerns observable behavior, it is, on the one hand, more specific than general risk factors, but on the other hand, it is a broader concept than a threat, because leaking behavior includes threats as well as other behaviors reflecting the individual's planning and preparation to carry out a violent act.

Leaking has been observed prior to every school shooting in Germany[24] and in most of the international cases, for the most part repeatedly and in detail.[25] This suggests that leaking may be a valuable starting point for preventive measures. However, there has been little research on the characteristics of leaking, its frequency (base rate), or reliable indicators for its seriousness.[26] Furthermore, because it is a relatively new concept that has not received much attention in education, teachers and other school personnel may not be prepared to recognize, assess, and respond to leaking adequately.

Programs to train professionals in the identification of risk factors have been used successfully in other prevention efforts, such as the prevention of suicide.[27] Thus, a pilot study was conducted in order to train teachers to identify and report leaking behavior among students in eight schools in Berlin. In each of these schools we conducted a thirty-to-sixty-minute informational meeting. Teachers were introduced to the project, and they were informed about leaking, risk factors for school shootings, and emergency guidelines. They were instructed to choose a "leaking appointee" from their faculty. The appointee was intended to function as a contact person for teachers witnessing leaking and/or threats and as a coordinator for collecting information about leaking. In addition, teachers were asked to report leaking incidents during a six-to-nine-month period.

Teachers completed a questionnaire after the informational meeting (T1) and after the reporting period six to nine months later (T2). The questionnaire contained questions about the informational meeting, the teachers' prior knowledge about leaking (only at T1), their knowledge about appropriate actions in such cases, their awareness and knowledge about the emergency guidelines, their subjective confidence in their decisions and actions concerning leaking and threats, and concerns and expectations regarding the use of a leaking appointee. A total of 239 teachers answered the questionnaire at T1 and 166 at T2, with 81 teachers answering at both times.

The results[28] may be summarized as follows: Teachers reported few concerns about informing staff of the Berlin Leaking Project about leaking incidents. During the six-to-nine-month period, only three incidents were actually reported, although in the questionnaire at least one teacher from each of the eight schools admitted having witnessed at least one incident during this period. On the one hand, it seems as if some incidents of leaking were not reported and the exact frequency remains unclear. On the other hand, there seems to be a manageable amount of leaking at schools, which makes individual interventions feasible.

Most teachers evaluated the informational meeting positively. They reported feeling less worried and reported a richer repertoire of reactions to leaking, as well as increased knowledge of the emergency guidelines. After some initial skepticism, teachers accepted the idea of keeping a leaking appointee at their school. Despite these improvements, teachers also reported feelings of insecurity about their ability to assess leaking and expressed a strong wish for further support from the police and school psychologists.

In conclusion, the pilot study indicated that teachers had little knowledge of leaking and other risk factors, but were open and receptive to instruction in a brief training session. It also seemed that they responded best to interactive training sessions accompanied by practical examples.[29]

NETWASS—A situational approach to indicated prevention

The NETWASS project is based on international research on school shootings, findings of the Berlin Leaking Project, and analysis of the legal and administrative conditions in the German states.[30] NETWASS uses a threat assessment approach[31] and draws on first evaluations of this strategy in U.S. schools.[32]

Why does NETWASS focus on early specific intervention?

Retrospective analyses of school shootings suggest that the offenses did not happen abruptly, but rather that perpetrators had been on a developmental pathway to violence that may include a multitude of interacting factors.[33] Although these pathways are not well understood, plans for violent acts arise when students have painful experiences and crises, so that early detection and provision of suitable help is necessary.

Accordingly, the main objective of the NETWASS project is the early, but indicated, prevention of school shootings and severe targeted school violence. This prevention approach addresses (1) threats and leaking, and (2) psychosocial risk factors. Combining the assessment of behavior with the assessment of psychosocial risk factors can be regarded as a highly valuable strategy for early detection and prediction.[34] The intervention is typically initiated after teachers report incidents of leaking. Students also may observe leaking,[35] so the NETWASS project will encourage teachers to foster an atmosphere of trust between students and staff. Students will not be asked to observe their peers or to practice "snitching," but will be encouraged to share possible concerns and seek help for students who seem to be troubled. They will be taught that some students might express a cry for help through their troubling behavior.

The core approach is to enhance teachers' awareness and attentiveness, and to strengthen the feelings of responsibility among teachers and students. Moreover, the basic idea of this prevention approach is not to stigmatize a potential perpetrator, but to become aware of a troubled student who needs support, protection, and encouragement.

The NETWASS threat assessment and early warning system at schools

It did not seem feasible to directly adopt the U.S. approach to threat assessment for several reasons. Germany has a trinomial, differentiated school system and different staffing patterns and responsibilities for school psychologists.[36] Furthermore, schools in Germany do not have school resource officers like many schools in the United States. Finally, the formal emergency guidelines in Germany require the development of a threat assessment system specific to the situation at schools in the different German states.

The NETWASS threat assessment and early warning system works like a filter in which information is collected and brought together at a central place. It functions as a filter insofar that only the most serious cases are passed forward for threat assessment. The NETWASS threat assessment and early warning system starts out with threats and incidents of violence against others or self, possible leakage, and risk factors (see Figure 4.1).

Teachers are asked to report incidents to the central "prevention appointee." At every process step, it is possible to undertake a standard pedagogic reaction or an immediate safety measure

Figure 4.1. NETWASS threat assessment system–process steps

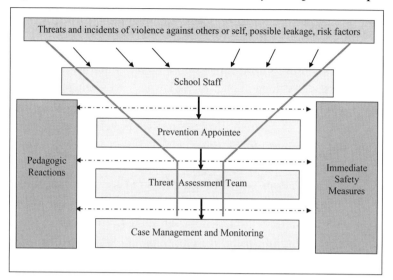

according to needs of the case. This approach differs from the Virginia model for threat assessment[37] because teachers are asked to consider not only threats, but also other forms of conspicuous behavior that could be signs of leaking, like intensive preoccupation with violence, weapons, and past school shootings. Additionally, teachers should look for a coincidence of several risk factors such as social isolation, rejection, or experiences of loss. They are asked to report all incidents they become aware of, except those that are clearly explainable or easily resolved, similar to the definition of transient threats by Cornell and others.[38] Teachers need not report incidents that imply no sustained intention to harm somebody, misunderstood humor, or situational expression of anger, when followed by an apology.[39]

Also similar to the Virginia model, the school principal takes responsibility as the central contact person, which we call the prevention appointee, but the principal may delegate this task to a formally selected and trained teacher. The prevention appointee will collect reports by his or her colleagues. If the appointee needs additional information or is in doubt, he or she will decide to call the threat assessment team into action. The team consists of the school principal, the prevention appointee, and possibly other staff who know the student of concern, such as the homeroom teacher or a social worker. As police officers in Germany are obliged to file a charge as soon as they become aware of any statutory offense, schools may be reluctant to notify a law enforcement representative immediately. The NETWASS approach encourages schools to include a law enforcement professional on the threat assessment team, but leaves it up to the principal to decide whether to involve the police immediately or later in the process.

School psychologists are also members of the threat assessment team, but they may not be able to participate in all cases because of their assignment to multiple schools. In some of the German states (for example, Berlin), there are school psychologists with special expertise in violence prevention and conflict management who can support threat assessment efforts. For this reason, we leave it to the school and the school psychologist to determine when to involve them in a threat assessment.

Threat assessment decisions should be made by the team, even if the team leader has the formal authority to make decisions (for example, in case of disagreement). Therefore, interdisciplinary team building is an important aspect of our threat assessment training.

After conducting the threat assessment, the school will initiate appropriate interventions. Part of the NETWASS approach is to initiate regional professional networks of school psychologists, law enforcement personnel, youth welfare officers, and mental health professionals. Schools will be able to turn to these networks for help. Additionally, it is planned to install a phone help line providing schools with contacts for professional advice. After initiating support for the student, and in many cases for his or her family as well, the school has mainly the task of monitoring the process.

As noted previously, five out of twelve German school shootings were committed by former students who failed school and were suspended. Obviously, it is difficult or even impossible for school staff to observe leaking after a student has left school, but case studies[40] suggest that leaking occurred before the student dropped out. These cases underscore the need for school authorities to consider carefully the mental health and emotional status of students facing suspension. Schools may want to establish case management plans for students before and after a student is suspended from school and also install a phone help line for people outside of schools.

Training and evaluation study design

The ongoing training project and evaluation study comprise four training groups. First, school staff will be trained in a three-hour session to recognize and address leaking and other early warning signs that a student is on a potential pathway to severe targeted school violence. Second, the threat assessment team will be trained in a two-day workshop covering evaluation and management procedures, early risk factors, threats, and leaking. Third, school psychologists and police officers will be trained to carry out training for other threat assessment teams and thus cascade the program to a larger group of school staff. We want to determine whether this "train the trainers" approach is effective, because it would be a more efficient way to attain nationwide implementation. Finally, telephone counselors will be trained to work on the phone help line.

The comparative training design also includes different modes of intervention delivery. We compare self-instruction based on a brochure (comparison group), guided e-learning, and face-to-face-training conducted by NETWASS staff or by external trainers, and investigate which mode is most effective.

The main aims of the study are to evaluate the feasibility of the measures (whether they were implemented as planned), the implementation processes (how they were implemented), and the effectiveness (what impact the training had). To evaluate the effects of the four different training models, a quasi-experimental comparison group design will be used. Schools will be assigned to different types of training and assessed at three measurement points: pre-training, post-training, and nine-month follow-up.

The models will be implemented in more than 100 schools in three federal states representing a cross section of the German population: Berlin, representing the urban part of Germany; Brandenburg, a rural and less densely populated state; and the densely populated Baden-Wurttemberg. The selected schools will include approximately 5,000 teachers and 30,000 students. The sampling is structured as a stratified clustered sample. Three administrative school districts of each participating state have been selected for our evaluation study, varying in social and economic criteria (average household income, unemployment, and percentage of university graduates). The sampling also considers different school types within the differentiated German school system.

Teachers will be asked to complete a self-administered set of questionnaires at the three measurement points. The questionnaire measures personal experiences concerning school violence, self-efficacy, and school climate. Compliance will be assessed by periodic interviews with the prevention appointees and standardized documentation of every incident reported by school staff over the nine-month period. Student data will be collected in a separate survey designed to measure school climate, bullying experiences, and feelings of safety.

In addition to the principal objective of the NETWASS project—to determine which training approach is most effective—a second objective is to collect information on the nature and frequency of leaking in schools. This information could help improve research on the early detection of students on a possible pathway to violence. A third objective is to learn more about the connection between objective risks (percentage of leaking and threats that have not been carried out) and the subjective sense of safety by the participants.[41] The fourth and final objective is to determine whether schools will use the NETWASS structure and threat assessment model for other issues of concern, such as severe bullying incidents. This expanded use of the NETWASS system would promote its sustainability.

Conclusion

NETWASS fills a gap between universal violence prevention programs, such as schoolwide bullying prevention, character education, or discipline programs on the one hand, and immediate safety measures in cooperation with the police on the other. The NETWASS Project aims to encourage teachers' responsibility to recognize the development of their students and to notice when there are problems that deserve investigation and intervention. Enhancing teacher awareness is a core element of the NETWASS approach. Because students are more likely than teachers to observe leaking behavior, we will also train teachers to encourage their students to seek help and to share information about classmates that might be interpreted as a cry for help. The NETWASS project promotes the perspective that students should not be stigmatized as potential perpetrators, but viewed as young people experiencing a developmental problem or crisis that merits help.

Notes

1. Fein, R. A., Vossekuil, B., Pollack, W. S., Borum, R., Modzeleski, W., & Reddy, M. (2002). *Threat assessment in schools: A guide to managing threatening situations and to creating safe school climates.* Washington, DC: U.S. Secret Service, National Threat Assessment Center.

2. Vossekuil, B., Fein, R. A., Reddy, M., Borum, R., & Modzeleski, W. (2002). *The final report and findings of the Safe School Initiative: Implications for the prevention of school attacks in the United States.* Washington, DC: U.S. Secret Service and U.S. Department of Education.

3. Bondü, R., & Scheithauer, H. (2009). School shootings in Deutschland: Aktuelle Trends zur Prävention von schwerer zielgerichteter Gewalt an deutschen Schulen. *Praxis Kinderpsychologie und Kinderpsychiatrie, 58,* 685–701.

4. Senator für Bildung, Wissenschaft und Forschung. (2009). *Kleine Anfrage zur inneren Sicherheit.* Abgeordnetenhaus Berlin, 16. Wahlperiode, Drucksache 16/13549.

5. Landesregierung Baden-Württemberg. (2009). *Expertenkreis Amok: Gemeinsam handeln, Risiken erkennen und minimieren. Konsequenzen aus dem Amoklauf in Winnenden und Wendlingen am 11.März 2009.* Stuttgart.

6. Weapons law (WaffG), dated 10–11–2002 (BGBl. I S. 3970, 4592; 2003 I S. 1957), which is changed at last by the law of 07–17–2009, section 3, subsection 5 (BGBl. I S. 2062).

7. Schubarth, W. (2000). *Gewaltprävention in Schule und Jugendhilfe. Theoretische Grundlagen, empirische Ergebnisse, Praxismodelle*. Neuwied, Germany: Luchterhand.

8. For example, Bannenberg, B. (2010). *Amok. Ursachen erkenne—Warnsignale verstehen—Katastrophen verhindern*. Gütersloh, Germany: Gütersloher Verlagshaus.

9. Fein et al. (2002).

10. Cornell, D., & Sheras, P. (2006). *Guidelines for responding to student threats of violence*. Longmont, CO: Sopris West.

11. For example, Hahn, R., Fuqua-Whitley, D., Wethington, H., Lowy, J., Crosby, A., Fullilove, M., et al. (2007). Effectiveness of universal school-based programs to prevent violent and aggressive behavior. A systematic review. *American Journal of Preventive Medicine, 33*, 114–129.

12. Sewell, K. W., & Mendelsohn, M. (2000). Profiling potentially violent youth: Statistical and methodological problems. *Children's Services: Social Policy, Research, and Practice, 3*, 147–169; Reddy, M., Borum, R., Berglund, J., Vossekuil, B., Fein, R. A., & Modzeleski, W. (2001). Evaluating risk for targeted violence in schools: Comparing risk assessment, threat assessment, and other approaches. *Psychology in the Schools, 38*, 157–172; Vossekuil et al. (2002).

13. Lange, T., & Greve, W. (2002). Amoklauf in der Schule—Allgemeine Überlegungen aus speziellem Anlass. *Soziale Probleme, 13*, 80–101.

14. Lange & Greve. (2002); Bannenberg. (2010).

15. Scheithauer, H., & Bondü, R. (2009). *Amok. Wissen was stimmt*. Freiburg im Breisgau, Germany: Herder.

16. O'Toole, M. E. (2000). *The school shooter: A threat assessment perspective*. Quantico, VA: National Center for the Analysis of Violent Crime, Federal Bureau of Investigation; Cornell, D. (2006). *School violence. Fears versus facts*. Mahwah, NJ: Lawrence Erlbaum.

17. Cornell, D., Sheras, P., Gregory, A., & Fan, X. (2009). A retrospective study of school safety conditions in high schools using the Virginia threat assessment guidelines versus alternative approaches. *School Psychology Quarterly, 24*, 119–129.

18. Fox, C., & Harding, D. J. (2005). School shootings as organizational deviance. *Sociology of Education, 78*, 69–97.

19. Cornell & Sheras. (2006).

20. Cornell et al. (2009).

21. Fein et al. (2002).

22. O'Toole. (2000).

23. Bondü, R. (2010). *School shootings in Deutschland. Internationaler Vergleich, Warnsignale, Risikofaktoren, Entwicklungsverläufe* (Unpublished doctoral dissertation). Department of Education and Psychology, Freie Universität, Berlin, Germany.

24. Bondü. (2010).

25. Moore, M. H., Petrie, C. V., Braga, A. A., & McLaughlin, B. L. (Eds.). (2003). *Deadly lessons. Understanding lethal school violence*. Washington, DC: National Academic Press; Newman, K., Fox, C., Harding, D. J., Mehta, J., &

Roth, W. (2004). *Rampage. The social roots of school shootings.* New York: Perseus Books; Vossekuil et al. (2002).

26. Moore et al. (2003).

27. For example, Chagnon, F., Houle, J., Marcoux, I., & Renaud, J. (2007). Control-group study of an intervention training program for youth suicide prevention. *Suicide and Life-Threatening Behavior, 37,* 135–144.

28. Bondü, R., & Scheithauer, H. (2011).*Treating serious threats by students: A pilot study in German schools.* Manuscript in preparation.

29. Bondü & Scheithauer. (2011).

30. See Bondü, Cornell, & Scheithauer, this issue.

31. Fein et al. (2002).

32. Cornell et al. (2009); Cornell, D., Sheras, P. L., Kaplan, S., McConville, D., Douglass, J., Elkon, A., et al. (2004). Guidelines for student threat assessment: Field-test findings. *School Psychology Review, 33,* 527–546.

33. Heubrock, D., Hayer, T., Rusch, S., & Scheithauer, H. (2005). Prävention von schwerer zielgerichteter Gewalt an Schulen—Rechtspsychologische und kriminalpräventive Ansätze. *Polizei & Wissenschaft, 1/2005,* 43–57.

34. Scheithauer, H., & Petermann, F. (2002). Prädiktion aggressiv/dissozialen Verhaltens: Entwicklungsmodelle, Risikobedingungen und multiple-gating-screening. *Zeitschrift für Gesundheitspsychologie, 10,* 121–140.

35. Gasser, K. H., Creuzfeldt, M., Näher, M., Rainer, R., & Wickler, P. (2004). *Bericht der Kommission Gutenberg-Gymnasium.* Erfurt, 371.

36. In Germany, each school district provides a team of school psychologists, responsible for all schools in their district. In some rural areas, there is only one school psychologist responsible for 10,000 students.

37. Cornell et al. (2004).

38. Cornell & Sheras. (2006).

39. Cornell et al. (2004).

40. Gasser et al. (2004).

41. Cornell. (2006).

VINCENZ LEUSCHNER *is the coordinator of the NETWASS project and currently working at Freie Universität Berlin.*

REBECCA BONDÜ *has been the coordinator of the Berlin Leaking Project and is currently working at Ruhr-Universität Bochum.*

MIRIAM SCHROER-HIPPEL *is currently working in the NETWASS Project at Freie Universität Berlin.*

JENNIFER PANNO *is currently working in the NETWASS Project at Freie Universität Berlin.*

NEW DIRECTIONS FOR YOUTH DEVELOPMENT • DOI: 10.1002/yd

KATHARINA NEUMETZLER *is currently working in the* NETWASS *Project at Freie Universität Berlin.*

SARAH FISCH *is currently working in the* NETWASS *Project at Freie Universität Berlin.*

JOHANNA SCHOLL *is currently working in the* NETWASS *Project at Freie Universität Berlin.*

HERBERT SCHEITHAUER *is professor for developmental psychology and clinical psychology at Freie Universität Berlin, and director of the Berlin Leaking Project and the* NETWASS *Project.*

The Swiss justice system focuses on violence prevention through early detection and intervention.

5

Procedures for preventing juvenile violence in Switzerland: The Zurich model

Jérôme Endrass, Astrid Rossegger,
Frank Urbaniok, Arja Laubacher,
Christine Schnyder Pierce, Konstantin Moskvitin

THE PENAL CODE IN Switzerland is strongly oriented toward the prevention of crime. Hence, most cases involving severe acts of violence trigger a psychiatric evaluation that includes a risk assessment. The threshold for court-ordered treatment is low and follows a rather pragmatic approach: On the basis of a psychiatric expert opinion, the court can order a specific therapeutic or confinement measure. Treatment can be ordered regardless of criminal responsibility. The court's decision depends upon the determined risk for reoffending and whether there are treatment strategies available to reduce this risk. In most cases, the courts order outpatient treatment that can follow a period of treatment

NEW DIRECTIONS FOR YOUTH DEVELOPMENT, NO. 129, SPRING 2011 © WILEY PERIODICALS, INC.
Published online in Wiley Online Library (wileyonlinelibrary.com) • DOI: 10.1002/yd.388

during incarceration, during a suspended sentence or period of probation, or even while awaiting sentencing.

The Swiss penal juvenile law

Although the Swiss penal code offers flexibility in risk management, there are some limitations when dealing with juvenile offenders.

Sentence limitations

The juvenile penal code covers ages ten to eighteen. Although the age of criminal responsibility begins at the age of ten, youth under the age of fifteen cannot be incarcerated, and juvenile offenders between fifteen and sixteen can be incarcerated for no more than one year. Juvenile offenders ages sixteen to eighteen at the time of the offense can be incarcerated no more than four years, even in the most severe cases. In addition, juvenile offenders must be provided with a high school or vocational curriculum in the institution.

Treatment ends at age twenty-two

A wide variety of interventions can be ordered by the court, including supervision (mostly by social workers), social work assistance for the family, and outpatient or inpatient psychiatric treatment. The court may sentence a young offender and simultaneously order treatment. If treatment is deemed successful, the sentence can be discontinued. However, all legal measures for young offenders are discontinued at age twenty-two, regardless of the success of treatment, the severity of the crime, or the risk for recidivism.

Four-year maximum institutionalization

Among young offenders (eighteen to twenty-five years old) a court-ordered inpatient social-therapeutic program can last a maximum of four years. Typically, this program takes place in a specialized,

PREVENTING JUVENILE VIOLENCE IN SWITZERLAND   81

low-security institution with offense-oriented treatment and vocational training. Even though the Swiss penal code originally
exempted violent juvenile offenders from these social-therapeutic
programs, it is now quite common for even very violent young
offenders to be court-ordered to participate in these programs.

Mass shooting by Friedrich Leibacher—Lessons learned

The homicide rate in Switzerland is quite low, approximately 0.83
per 100,000 inhabitants,[1] and there are no records of homicidal
school shootings. However, a mass shooting that occurred in
the aftermath of 9/11, known as the Zug massacre, is noteworthy
because it led to changes in how potentially violent adults
and juveniles are handled by the justice systems of several
cantons.

   On September 27, 2001, fifty-seven-year-old Friedrich Leibacher entered the cantonal parliament (similar to a state legislature in the United States) in Zug armed with an assault rifle, a
shotgun, a semiautomatic pistol, and homemade bombs. He immediately opened fire in the assembly hall, killing three members of
the executive council and eleven members of the cantonal parliament. Leibacher shot himself immediately after the killings and
left a suicide note in which he accused the cantonal authorities of
a plot against him. The mass shooting was the result of a three-
year conflict with authorities stemming from his belief that he was
unjustly treated by a public bus driver. Leibacher wrote letters of
complaint in which he uttered threats and accused the authorities
of a conspiracy against him. Multiple agencies of the cantonal
administration (for example, medical doctors who evaluated his
disability pension, the social security administration) were unsuccessful in de-escalating the conflict. Finally, the district attorney
pressed charges for uttering threats.

   A psychiatric expert opinion commissioned after the killings
concluded that, although Leibacher displayed very peculiar behavior long before the assault, the danger he presented did not

NEW DIRECTIONS FOR YOUTH DEVELOPMENT • DOI: 10.1002/yd

become clearly evident until all the information regarding his past and recent behavior was put together. The Zug massacre significantly changed how authorities in many cantons deal with persons who are perceived to be hostile or who utter threats. In such cases, the office of public prosecution now appoints a case manager to gather all available information and a forensic expert to assess the risk for violence and propose intervention strategies.

Zurich model

Among the twenty-six Swiss cantons, Zurich is perhaps the foremost oriented toward crime prevention.[2] The cantonal authorities dealing with offenders (for example, state penitentiary, prison services, juvenile detention and treatment centers, probation services, psychiatric/psychological services) are integrated through the office of corrections, which in turn collaborates with the office of public prosecution. For example, if an initial threat assessment by the office of public prosecution reveals a certain level of dangerousness, a forensic risk appraisal is completed by a forensic psychiatrist or psychologist from the office of corrections. The assessment always includes an opinion regarding risk for recidivism and recommendations for specific risk-management interventions.

When assessing the risk for recidivism, four main criteria are considered: psychopathology, such as antisocial, paranoid, or narcissistic personality disorders and schizophrenia spectrum disorders; behavioral dispositions, such as an affinity for weapons; form and content of the uttered threats, such as a specific target, method, or time; and protective factors, such as triggers to violent acts versus a preventive social network. For the risk assessment, the office of public prosecution provides all records at its disposal (testimonies of the accused, as well as the testimonies of the person threatened, teachers, and parents). Risk assessments almost always include an interview with the subject uttering the threats, but this person can choose to decline.

The recommended risk-management strategies are multifaceted and highly dependent on the needs of the offender. Often, one of the most relevant decisions is whether someone can be released from jail while awaiting trial. There may be recommendations regarding the conditions of the release (for example, participating in single or group treatment, taking neuroleptic medication). Recommendations can include psychiatric hospitalization, outpatient treatment, a monthly meeting with a social worker, or some combination of these options. Furthermore, the forensic expert could make recommendations for school personnel to monitor or respond to a student's threatening behavior.[3]

As an example of how the model works, consider the case of a student who utters threats to his teacher. In such a case, if the teacher considers the threat to be serious and wants the student to be prosecuted, the teacher has to notify the police. Following a police investigation, the office of public prosecution can open criminal proceedings and commission a forensic expert opinion. The forensic expert not only assesses the risk for physical violence, but also recommends intervention strategies. These may include, for example, a house search for weapons, confiscation of weapons, and restraining orders. In addition, the forensic expert is expected to opine about the youth's amenability to treatment and to recommend specific treatment modalities, programs, and settings.

Recently, a Swiss study evaluated the effectiveness of risk assessment by forensic experts of adults and juveniles who were charged with uttering threats and were due to be released from detention while awaiting trial. Of sixty-nine total cases, an early release was recommended for thirty-seven cases. Of these thirty-seven persons, only five committed a criminal offense within three years after release from prison, all of which involved minor assaults resulting in no serious injury to the victims. For all but two of the thirty-seven subjects, the recommendation for release was conditional on certain requirements, such as appointment of a case manager, participation in offense-oriented therapy, abstinence from illicit substances, compliance with psychiatric medication, or a ban from carrying a firearm.[4] However, conclusions should be interpreted with caution because it was not possible to use a control group in this study.

Case study

The following case study is based on a psychiatric evaluation by the Psychiatric/Psychological Service of the Zurich Criminal Justice System. R. was a young man of seventeen with a long history of problematic and delinquent behavior. He had his first contact with mental health professionals in kindergarten when he was assessed for motor and speech problems. His problems continued throughout primary school and he showed poor school performance. He had a tendency to lie and was a loner, awkward in social situations, and unable to deal with conflicts in a productive manner. These problems worsened as he grew older.

Since childhood, R. had been fascinated by fire and he committed his first arson at age five. Between ages thirteen and sixteen, he committed at least thirteen acts of arson, mostly because he wanted to see firefighters in action. Some of the arsons caused significant damage and endangered human lives, including one that caused roughly $500,000 in damages. At age fourteen, R. was treated for the first time in a psychiatric clinic because of agitation and dissociative symptoms. At age sixteen, he was hospitalized again for the same symptoms, and a diagnosis of borderline personality disorder was considered. During his inpatient treatment, R. left the ward several times without permission and committed further offenses, including arson, driving without a license, utterance of threats, and damage to property. He also showed a pattern of manipulative behavior and pathological lying; for example, it was proven by the office of public prosecution that he falsely accused his own brother of having sexually assaulted him over a period of years. R.'s parents were unwilling to comply with clinic recommendations, minimized his dangerous behavior, and tried to get him discharged from the hospital. The clinic called upon the guardianship authority to keep R. institutionalized.

NEW DIRECTIONS FOR YOUTH DEVELOPMENT • DOI: 10.1002/yd

The office of public prosecution requested that the office of correction complete a risk assessment during R.'s inpatient treatment after R. reported persistent homicidal fantasies toward his female therapist. The fantasies became more and more detailed and realistic. Furthermore, he reported that prior to the inpatient treatment he fell in love with his teacher and had started following her home. The hopelessness of his affection had led to homicidal fantasies toward her as well. In addition, R. had started to carry a knife to school.

R. was given the diagnoses of conduct disorder, antisocial personality disorder, and pathological fire setting. Because his violent behavior was judged to be instrumental rather than reactive, the provisional diagnosis of a borderline personality was ruled out. Although only seventeen years old, he received a very high score of 30 on the Psychopathy Checklist (PCL-R). His score reflected his impulsivity and pathological lying, as well as his lack of guilt, empathy, and ability to learn from punishment.[5] The forensic experts concluded that his risk for committing a severe violent offense was very high and, thus, recommended a court-ordered inpatient social-therapeutic program in a specialized institution with offense-oriented treatment and vocational training. Furthermore, the experts concluded that the lack of risk awareness by his parents and R.'s noncompliance with interventions meant that R. needed to be institutionalized in a secure environment. The court followed these recommendations.

Just a few weeks after being transferred to the juvenile detention center, R. set a fire in his room, and as a result was transferred to a prison because he was considered too dangerous to be kept anywhere else. Therapeutic interventions were continued at the prison. After several months R. was transferred back to the juvenile detention center. This time progress was more promising, as he stopped setting fires and uttering threats. He was able to participate in individual and group therapies, as well as occupational activities. Whether R.'s participation in the treatment plan of the juvenile detention center reflected a true improvement or was rather an adaption to the new environment remains unclear.

NEW DIRECTIONS FOR YOUTH DEVELOPMENT • DOI: 10.1002/yd

Conclusion

The low rate of violence, especially homicidal acts, in Switzerland, may be—at least partially—a result of the Swiss justice system's strong focus on violence prevention. Key factors of violence prevention are early detection and intervention, as well as tailored measures and intervention options. In Zurich, one of the most important factors contributing to violence prevention is the close cooperation between law-enforcement and risk-assessment specialists from the criminal-justice system, especially regarding the assessment of imminent danger in persons who utter threats. Experts from different agencies with different professional backgrounds work closely together to prevent violent acts. Although the Swiss justice system limits the use of long-term treatment for juveniles (beyond four years), it does allow for early and targeted intervention with potentially violent youths before they become violent. A full-scale, comprehensive evaluation of its effectiveness is merited.

Notes

1. Taveres, C., & Thomas, G. (2009). Population and social conditions. *Eurostat—Statistics in Focus, 36,* 1–11.
2. Urbaniok, F., Rossegger, A., Kherfouche, C., & Endrass, J. (2007). Validität von fokalen Risikoeinschätzungen und Interventionsempfehlungen bei Personen mit Anzeichen für kurz-bis mittelfristige Gefährlichkeit: Eine Evaluationsstudie des Zürcher Kurzgutachtenprojekts [Validity of focal risk assessments and recommended interventions of persons posing a short-to medium-term dangerousness: An evaluation study of the Zurich Brief Assessment Project]. *Schweizer Archiv für Neurologie und Psychiatrie, 158,* 107–114.
3. Urbaniok et al. (2007).
4. Urbaniok, F., Rinne, T., Held, L., Rossegger, A., & Endrass, J. (2008). Forensische Risikokalkulationen: Grundlegende methodische Aspekte zur Beurteilung der Anwendbarkeit und Validität verschiedener Verfahren [Forensic risk calculation: Basic methodological aspects for the evaluation of the applicability and validity of diverse methods]. *Fortschritte der Neurologie, Psychiatrie, 76,* 470–477.
5. Hare, R. (1991). *Manual for the revised psychopathy checklist.* Toronto, Canada: Multi-Health Systems.

JÉRÔME ENDRASS *is head of the research department at the Psychiatric/ Psychological Service (PPS) of the Zurich Office of Corrections.*

ASTRID ROSSEGGER *is a psychologist at the Psychiatric/Psychological Service (PPS) of the Zurich Office of Corrections.*

FRANK URBANIOK *is the director of the Psychiatric/Psychological Service (PPS) of the Zurich Office of Corrections.*

ARJA LAUBACHER *is a psychologist at the Psychiatric/Psychological Service (PPS) of the Zurich Office of Corrections.*

CHRISTINE SCHNYDER PIERCE *is an associate at the Psychological Consulting Services in Salem, Massachusetts. She is also a qualified examiner at the Forensic Health Services in Braintree, Massachusetts.*

KONSTANTIN MOSKVITIN *is attending psychiatrist at the Psychiatric/ Psychological Service (PPS) of the Zurich Office of Corrections.*

The success of school-based law enforcement requires careful selection and specialized training of officers who can adapt to the school culture and work cooperatively with school authorities.

6

The role of law enforcement in schools: The Virginia experience— A practitioner report

Steven Clark

IN THE LATE 1990s, as school shootings dominated the headlines in the United States, many states rushed to place law enforcement officers in schools. However, it was not long before it became apparent that traditional law enforcement training did not adequately prepare officers for work in schools. Officers who functioned efficiently and comfortably on the street were typically ill-prepared for the challenges faced by school-based law enforcement officers. Many officers had difficulty communicating and interacting with students, and there were conflicts with school administrators about authority and management issues. There were frequent questions about whether a student's misbehavior should be treated as a disciplinary matter or a crime. This article will summarize some of the typical challenges and potential problems faced by police officers assigned to schools, then describe the Virginia training program for school resource officers and some

NEW DIRECTIONS FOR YOUTH DEVELOPMENT, NO. 129, SPRING 2011 © WILEY PERIODICALS, INC.
Published online in Wiley Online Library (wileyonlinelibrary.com) • DOI: 10.1002/yd.389

recommended practices for successful partnerships between school and law enforcement authorities.

Some challenges of police work in schools

Police recruits ordinarily are trained in police academies to protect a clearly defined area of personal space for safety reasons. The new school resource officers (SROs) quickly found themselves surrounded and jostled by energetic young people who crowd the hallways when changing classes. Ordinarily, citizens in the community treat officers with courtesy and respect. In contrast, many young people laugh and joke, and are sometimes not respectful. Law enforcement officers are trained to maintain peace and order, elements that may be lacking in some challenging school environments. The typical school is populated by many boisterous young people. The noise level, congestion, and energy can be unsettling to an officer who is not prepared for this environment. In the early years of the school–police partnership, officers were sometimes surprised to find that the school administration did not welcome them with open arms. Often, a school administrator would interpret the assignment of a police officer to the school as a sign that the principal could not manage the students and had lost control. As the various school–police partnerships matured, these issues became less common.

A more persistent problem is that the school culture operates with two sets of rules that are often not clearly distinguished: the criminal code and the school's discipline code. The police officer is trained to enforce the criminal code and to follow standard procedures in determining whether someone has broken the law, to gather evidence regarding the crime, and to make an arrest in appropriate situations. Violations of the criminal code are serious matters and often leave little room for an officer to use discretion or consider less formal alternatives to arrest and prosecution. In contrast, school rules address a variety of behaviors that may or may not be violations of the law. For example, the SRO who

NEW DIRECTIONS FOR YOUTH DEVELOPMENT • DOI: 10.1002/yd

ignores dress code violations because they are not violations of the law soon finds that students are comfortable flaunting school violations because they perceive the SRO is powerless to enforce them. Although noncriminal behavior enforcement should not be the primary function of the SRO, it is always preferable that the SRO be given the authority by the principal to address school code-of-conduct violations. This assures that the students receive a consistent level of service from all of the adults that work in the school.

Another consistent area of confusion between SROs and school administrators involves the handling of typical student behaviors that on the street would be considered criminal in nature. An officer may observe a serious fight on campus that would meet the definition of a criminal act. The officer may be frustrated by resistance from the school administrator who wants no arrest and no charges, but simply a three-day suspension from school. This puts the SRO in an awkward situation. To defy the principal would seriously jeopardize their important relationship. However, to follow the principal's wishes would be neglecting the oath of every officer sworn to uphold the law. Such relationships between SROs and school administrators are understandably fragile. School administrators may resist the authority of the SRO when an arrest is required and the SRO may resent what seems from the SRO's perspective to be interference by a school administrator in a police matter. The best-case scenario is one in which the SRO welcomes suggestions from the school administrator prior to making the determination of how a crime is to be handled. In many situations in the United States, officers have broad discretion to determine the most appropriate response to a possible criminal act. If an arrest and criminal charge are necessary, there are still options that may be preferable to a regular court process that results in a permanent criminal record. In Virginia, many first-time offenders can have their case handled unofficially within the juvenile court system. In these situations, the youth and parents will agree with a court-ordered consequence that may include restitution of damages, counseling, or community service assignments. If the youth successfully completes the assigned tasks, the criminal prosecution will not proceed and there will be no permanent criminal record of the offense. SRO programs often progressed through years of difficult development as school administrators, police administrators, students, staff, and faculty all learned to operate as a team rather than individuals with competing interests.

What gradually emerged was a unique law enforcement role that has been embraced by a select group of law enforcement specialists who thrive on campuses in Virginia and throughout the country. The SRO is no longer viewed as simply a uniformed presence on campus tasked with keeping the peace and arresting lawbreakers. If a school division wishes to utilize a police officer for this limited purpose, it is clearly more economical and efficient to simply detain the offender and wait for a police officer to respond, as is typically done in all other areas of the community.

The Virginia training program for SROs

Virginia was one of the first states to recognize the need to train and prepare officers for the demands and challenges of working in schools. In 1999, the Virginia legislature created the Virginia Center for School Safety as a state entity responsible for training law enforcement officers to serve in schools. To emphasize the special training and skills required of these officers, they were termed school resource officers. There is now a National Association of School Resource Officers with more than 6,000 members.[1]

Over the past twenty years, the number of SROs in Virginia has grown to the point that 559 of 631 Virginia secondary schools have an officer on duty at all times when school is in session.[2] This includes middle schools (students ages 11 to 13 in grades 6–8) and high schools (ages 14 to 17 in grades 9–12). The Center also trains security officers who do not have full police authority. Recently, the Center has been mandated to train officers who work in college and university settings, too.

Unfortunately, there is no approved model of training; nor are there national standards for school-based law enforcement officer training. Virginia's SRO training program has undergone a continual evolution over the past fifteen years. Today, a typical Virginia SRO training program consists of forty hours of instruction in topics that include legal and liability issues of school-based law enforcement, critical incident planning and response, homeland security for schools, substance abuse and suicide prevention, gang identification and prevention, crime prevention through environmental design, conflict mediation, Internet crime, bullying prevention, law-related educational programs, and techniques for dealing with confrontational parents and students.

SRO program recommendations

Many of the problems for new SROs and those schools that wish to utilize them can be avoided by carefully exploring the ways in which the SRO should or should not be utilized on campus. To have the greatest chance of success, the SRO's role on campus should be carefully spelled out in a detailed memorandum of understanding (MOU) that is approved by the top levels of both the law enforcement agency and the school system.[3] Within this foundational document, the supervisory structure to oversee the program should be clearly explained. In most cases, the law enforcement supervisor will be responsible for direct supervision, scheduling, and evaluation of the SRO. The MOU should give ample opportunity for input from the school administrators who manage the school. Dispute resolution procedures should be carefully planned to ensure that the problems and disagreements that will surely occur are quickly and reasonably resolved. The document should also clearly outline the boundaries of the SRO services to the school. This will prevent friction should the SRO be assigned to duties that are not consistent with the mission of the police department. For example, it is generally considered poor police procedure to assign an officer to the same location at the same time each school day. For officer safety and utmost effectiveness, an officer's movements should not follow a consistent pattern or time schedule. However, many school administrators wish for the SRO to be stationed at a particular problem area for a specified time each day. With a clear MOU and an appreciation of the valid concerns of both the police and the school administrator, suitable compromises can be found.

One troublesome area that should be addressed by the MOU is the sharing of the SRO's time between the school system and the police department.[4] Schools tend to take ownership of their SRO and when an effective SRO is absent for days or sometimes weeks at a time, the school administration can be understandably concerned about their missing officer. A detailed MOU will outline the various situations that will necessitate the officer being absent from the campus. With court appearances, mandated training, and sometimes simply the need to fill in on patrol to maintain minimum staffing levels, schools should understand that the SRO is first and foremost an employee of the police department and the needs of the police department will usually supersede the needs of the school.

The SRO should focus primarily on crime prevention through two recognized law enforcement strategies: crime prevention through environmental design (CPTED) and community-oriented policing. CPTED involves the evaluation of common problem areas such as parking lots, cafeterias, or locker rooms, so that officers can assist administrators and faculty in finding creative and cost-effective ways of addressing these problems. It is a process that uses simple lighting, landscaping, and behavioral management techniques to contribute to a safer setting.

Common community policing practices stress the importance of officers taking the initiative to become integrated and engaged with the community (in this case the school) that they serve. By reaching out to community members, being friendly and approachable, and seeking to develop healthy partnerships with key community members, the SRO can quickly assess and respond to problem issues that impact the safety of the school community. The SRO should soon be viewed as part of the school family, and not just an outsider who arrests people. Once an officer is accepted as a member of the school community, there is a great opportunity for the officer to become a multifaceted resource for the entire school. Most SROs have received specialized training in these areas and are skilled at both CPTED and community policing.

The SRO should capitalize on any opportunity to interact with students both inside and outside of the classroom. Many SROs have volunteered as athletic coaches or tutors in order to interact with students outside of the traditional law enforcement role. There are now a wide variety of free lesson plans and custom courses that are designed especially for law enforcement officers working in schools. Within Virginia, many officers use Virginia Rules, a program designed by the Virginia Office of the Attorney General. This program is designed to teach students the key areas of the law that are most likely to affect a student in Virginia. Students are educated regarding specific laws dealing with substance abuse, driving, school attendance, violence, gangs, and weapons. Potential problem areas such as dating violence, parental rights and responsibilities, computer crime, and social networking issues are also addressed.

The SRO should seek to interact with as many parents as possible. In the course of their typical security and crowd control duties at sporting events, recitals, drama presentations, and graduation ceremonies, officers have the opportunity to interact with the parents of the children they serve. When the SRO has developed a prior relationship with the extended family members of a student, the parent is more likely to understand and appreciate the efforts of the SRO to keep students safe, even if that means their child's behavior may occasionally come under scrutiny.

The SRO should carefully document ongoing interactions with students. In the day-to-day life of the SRO, the officer may interact individually with many students. Although these interactions will generally not rise to the seriousness of requiring a police report or referral to school administration, officers should keep a personal record of all occurrences and interactions that they deem noteworthy. These records may assist the SRO in providing services to students who reveal a consistent pattern of behaviors that indicate possible substance abuse or other hazardous actions. For example, an officer who speaks to a boy about suspicious bruises should note the date of the interaction and the explanation given. If this officer finds the same child with the same type of injuries three weeks later, the officer can compare the explanation given by the boy with the officer's previous notes. Seemingly minor contacts with students can often reveal potentially serious situations that might otherwise seem unconnected. Relying simply on police reports to document the SRO's activities leaves valuable information undocumented.

In determining which cases the SRO should be involved in and to what extent, school administrators and faculty must remember that the SRO's primary mission is to enhance the safety, order, and discipline within the school by utilizing a skill set that involves experience in law enforcement, conflict mediation, safety-related education, and critical incident response. Officers have latitude to be involved in other matters that are typically faculty or administrative functions, but care must be taken to ensure that officers do not begin to act as agents of the school administration. Ordinary cases of bullying that do not result in serious physical injury to anyone are usually handled by the school administration and counseling staff. If the act of bullying also involved a serious criminal act, such as robbery, extortion, or physical injury to a victim, then the SRO would become involved.

Another area of concern is a search for prohibited materials such as weapons or drugs. As law enforcement officers, SROs cannot conduct searches unless certain legal requirements (probable cause) are met. In contrast, the U.S. courts permit school authorities greater latitude in deciding when to search a student or a student's locker.

The SRO should be prepared to act as the resident crisis response specialist on campus. Because officers are experienced at responding to critical incidents, this is one area in which the SRO can be a great resource to the school administrators. Schools have detailed crisis management plans that must be regularly reviewed and updated. However, most campuses lack a dedicated staff or faculty member with specialized training in emergency response procedures. The school's crisis response team can be strengthened by adding the SRO: an individual who has received specialized training and quite likely has personal experience in responding to a wide variety of critical incidents.

Finally, in the unlikely event of a crisis involving a school shooting, the SRO can play a critical role. Most of the North American school shooters have been suicidal male students who entered the school intending to kill others and then kill themselves. The window of opportunity during which the potential shooter can be engaged and intercepted is brief, typically a matter of several minutes. The presence of an armed and trained law enforcement officer who can respond instantly to the scene of the crime can be critical in saving lives.

SRO program challenges

One difficulty related to SRO programs is that the benefits of assigning police officers to schools are difficult to prove. Just as it is difficult for patrol officers to prove they prevented crimes through their patrols, an SRO program's effectiveness in reducing crime is also difficult to quantify.

Studies of the Virginia SRO programs over the past dozen years have shown that they are generally popular with the parents, staff, faculty, and students, but more rigorous empirical evidence is lacking. A well-funded national effort to measure the effectiveness of SROs in schools encountered insurmountable obstacles and ended in failure.[5]

A 2002 survey of 300 Virginia SROs revealed the most common challenges to SRO effectiveness. The greatest hindrance, identified by 37 percent of the surveyed officers, was teachers and administrators who either intentionally fail to report criminal acts to the SRO or were perceived by the SROs to be uncooperative or meddlesome. It is critical for officers and administrators to have a shared understanding of the boundary between a school disciplinary violation and a criminal matter.

SROs should have a clear understanding that they report to a law enforcement authority rather than the school administrator as their supervisor. The law enforcement supervisor with direct responsibility for oversight of the SRO usually spends little time on campus. It is therefore essential that the SRO's police supervisor maintain regular contact with school administrators to assess the officer's progress throughout the school year accurately.

SROs typically walk a fine line between serving the school administrators and serving their police department supervisor(s). As difficult as it may be to serve two masters effectively, the best programs are typically those where the police chief, the superintendent of schools, the principals, the SRO supervisor(s), and the SROs all know the clearly defined chain of command and the clearly defined dispute resolution process. Regular meetings between high-level police and school division managers can resolve many disputes before they escalate. The Virginia experience has shown that, at least once per school year, executive-level representatives of both the police department and the school system should meet to discuss their program goals and assess their progress. Additional meetings may be necessary to discuss high-profile incidents or complaints that may occur. SROs are law enforcement officers who happen to serve primarily within a school community.

The top SRO programs in Virginia are those in which the officers are well-trained for their transition to school-based law enforcement and carefully selected for this critical role. Ideally, the selection process for a new SRO should be sufficiently rigorous to disqualify candidates with undesirable qualities such as a quick temper, impatience, profane language, dishonesty, or any type of substance abuse issues. If possible, the school system should be actively involved in the selection process. The presence of one or two school administrators on the SRO selection panel is highly desirable. The best SROs are typically stable and calm, and demonstrate a natural aptitude and interest in working with young people. They will often be involved in various youth programs or youth sports teams in their communities. A skilled SRO requires patience, a good sense of humor, and a casual friendliness that makes the officer approachable. Officers lacking these qualities may find it difficult to gain acceptance by the staff, students, and parents.

The most highly regarded SRO programs are those that do not shuffle SROs unnecessarily. Experience has shown that it will usually take at least six months, if not a full school year, for the SRO to become comfortable and effective in this unique role. Departments that consistently swap SROs from school to school, or year to year, deprive the school and the SRO of the opportunity to build a healthy relationship. Without this relationship, the SRO has no real connection to the school community and typically functions in the role of enforcer. Officers functioning in this capacity have little to contribute to the school family and will rarely be successful in their assignment. Ideally, a capable SRO should be given a three-year term in a school. This length of assignment allows the officer to become fully integrated into the school family and develop meaningful relationships with students, faculty, and staff that are the common traits that connect all successful SROs. Longer terms run the risk of alienating the SRO from the employing law enforcement agency. For these reasons, the three-year term seems best suited to the SRO position.

The SRO should not be isolated from law enforcement supervision. The SRO supervisor can often make or break an SRO program. The effective supervisor will seek ways to recognize the SRO despite the fact that most of the SRO's work cannot be simply calculated by adding up arrests or citations. The diligent SRO supervisor will regularly meet with the principal and the SRO on the campus to be updated on areas of concern. Regular meetings between the SRO's law enforcement supervisor and the principal can also address potential problems or personality conflicts that can arise between the school administration and the SRO. Clear lines of communication and regular, informal meetings can keep these distractions to a minimum. Inattentive supervisors with little or no interest in school safety should never be put in charge of the SRO program. This type of supervisor can quickly undermine a

program and will guarantee that the best (and most suitable) officers will avoid the SRO position. The SRO who has an engaged
and knowledgeable supervisor can count on a fair evaluation and
the recognition the officer deserves for effectively serving in a
most challenging environment.

The school environment is unique in the world of law enforcement. It requires abilities that are sometimes viewed as liabilities in
other areas of law enforcement. SROs often become attached to
their school and their students. Although this makes them a better
SRO, an emotional attachment to those being served can often
lead to disappointment when the SRO is eventually reassigned.
Conversely, many SROs find that successfully completing a three-
year term in an active school setting is a great boost for their
resumes, often contributing to a future promotion. SROs that can
adapt to juggling the needs of parents, challenging students, staff,
faculty, and administrators and balance all of this with the skill of
being an impartial, friendly, and fair law enforcement officer are
often destined for more responsibility and promotion when they
return from their school assignment.

The SRO position should never be used to punish officers or as
a place to hide poorly performing or injured officers. Some locali-
ties have regrettably learned that a poorly functioning law enforcement officer is a costly liability within a school. If an officer
struggles to perform acceptably in a patrol function, how can one
expect this officer to excel when he or she is under a microscope
being carefully observed by hundreds of sometimes unpredictable
and emotional young people, as well as teachers, administrators,
and other school staff members? Assigning unsuitable officers as
SROs will usually end up embarrassing both the police department
and the school. This can be avoided if both the police chief and the
superintendent of schools agree on a rigorous selection process
that includes input from both school officials and the typical police
competitive selection process.

With the continuing threat of terrorism, armed intruders, and
the day-to-day challenges of maintaining safety, order, and discipline on campus, the SRO has become a true multifaceted resource

to schools in both urban and rural settings. The skillful SRO balances a genuine love for children with the commitment to promote safety, order, and discipline in school. The desire for safer schools drives improvements and advances in technology, teaching, architecture, administration, and even parenting. Virginia has found that the desire for safer schools has led to the evolution of this specialized law enforcement officer who has become an integral piece of the complex school safety puzzle.

Notes

1. Schuiteman, J. (2005). A national assessment of school resource officers. In *SRO Program Evaluation issues plus new commonsense findings*. Richmond, VA: Virginia Department of Criminal Justice Services. Retrieved from http://gwired.gwu.edu/hamfish/AnnualConference/2005

2. National Association of School Resource Officers. (n.d.). Retrieved from http://www.nasro.org/mc/page.do?sitePageId=115971&orgId=naasro

3. Virginia Department of Criminal Justice Services. (2002). *Virginia school resource officer: Facts II. Findings from the Spring 2002 canvass of Virginia law enforcement agencies*. Richmond, VA: Author. Retrieved from http://www.dcjs.virginia.gov/cple/grants/sro/facts2.pdf

4. The Virginia Center for School Safety, Department of Criminal Justice Services. (n.d.). *Model policy for school resource officers*. Richmond, VA: Author. Retrieved from http://www.dcjs.virginia.gov/cple/grants/sro/sroModelPolicy.pdf

5. Schuiteman. (2005).

STEVEN CLARK *coordinates training, resources, and technical assistance for the Virginia Center for School Safety and the Office of Campus Policing and Security at the Virginia Department of Criminal Justice Services.*

Safe2Tell®, proposed by the Columbine Commission, is an anonymous, 24/7 reporting system for receiving and forwarding threats of violence.

7

Safe2Tell®: An anonymous, 24/7 reporting system for preventing school violence

Susan R. T. Payne, Delbert S. Elliott

SHORTLY AFTER THE Columbine shooting in 1999, the governor of Colorado created the Columbine Review Commission,[1] charging the Commission with the responsibility of identifying the lessons that Columbine taught. The report of the Columbine Commission notes that the shooters, Eric Harris and Dylan Klebold, left a roadmap of red flags during the eighteen months before the shooting, for example, a hateful Web site, disturbing school essays and videos, arrest and participation in a sheriff's department diversion program, threats against another student, reports of bomb making, and a search warrant for the Harris home that was never served. A number of different people were aware that Harris and Klebold were involved in significant problems and questionable activities. It is also clear that friends of Harris and Klebold were involved in or aware of some of their preparation for that event. There were many signs that were ignored, or at least were not acted upon. But it is also true that no one in a

NEW DIRECTIONS FOR YOUTH DEVELOPMENT, NO. 129, SPRING 2011 © WILEY PERIODICALS, INC.
Published online in Wiley Online Library (wileyonlinelibrary.com) • DOI: 10.1002/yd.390

position of authority was aware of all of these signs prior to the event.

The Commission also observed that there was a code of silence at Columbine High School, a culture in which loyalty to friends overrode responsibility to report potential harmful behavior. Some students had critical information or knowledge that could have led to an official inquiry, but they did not share that information; they did not want to tattle on another student. Threats were not taken seriously, and there is evidence that Harris and Klebold were the victims of bullying, even though some school officials deny that. They were both marginalized in the school's culture, and there was inconsistent enforcement of the rules by the school.

In light of these findings, the Commission recommended the establishment of an anonymous reporting system whereby students and others could contact authorities to share concerns about potential threats of violence or other harmful behavior. This recommendation was reinforced by the U.S. Secret Service study[2] on targeted school shootings that found attackers made plans and that they nearly always talked about those plans with others. In 81 percent of these shootings, someone other than the attacker, typically friends or peers, knew of the plan but did not report it.

As described in this article, what we learned over a period of years in Colorado is that a stand-alone hotline is less than effective. However, an implemented program supported by laws that provide for information sharing and anonymous reporting with education and awareness, early intervention, and prevention, along with accountability and follow-up, provides a complete system where students feel they can report in a way that keeps them safe.

The Safe2Tell® reporting system

In response to the Commission's report, the Safe2Tell® statewide reporting system was established in 2003 with a grant from the Colorado Trust. Safe2Tell® is a public–private partnership under the leadership of the Colorado Attorney General. Special Agent

Susan Payne is the founding director and serves in this role as a state law enforcement official and a staff member of the Attorney General. Safe2Tell® has federal government status as a nonprofit [501(C)3] organization governed by a multidisciplinary, volunteer board of directors. The mission of Safe2Tell® is to ensure that all Colorado students, parents, teachers, and community members have access to a safe and anonymous way to report any concerns about their safety or the safety of others, with a focus on early intervention and prevention through awareness and education.

Tips are reported anonymously by a phone call to a toll-free number answered live twenty-four hours a day/seven days a week by trained communications officers from the Colorado State Patrol. Additionally, they can submit a tip through a Web reporting feature utilizing technology that permits two-way dialogue, but is anonymous and encrypted. Colorado is currently piloting a two-way texting feature in Jefferson County School District that involves 161 schools and 85,000 students. There are no answering machines, voicemail, or caller ID used. All information is taken seriously, and appropriate action is taken in response to credible information. Should the communications officer have reason to believe that the call is a prank call or false report, he or she is trained to interact with the caller to screen and assess the validity of the caller's report. With each report received information is immediately forwarded to one or more local school officials, mental health professionals, or law enforcement agencies as appropriate for their investigation and intervention. Safe2Tell® takes the extra step of following up with the agencies that receive the report to ensure that it was investigated, that action was taken, and that the outcome was tracked. This is done by the agency completing an on-line confidential disposition form indicating how the situation was handled. It is the school's responsibility to determine whether the information they are given in the Safe2Tell® report is valid, and then to report back.

The Safe2Tell® initiative is unique in three ways: the anonymity of callers is legally protected, there is follow-up on calls to document what action was taken, and there is an extensive educational component designed to empower students and encourage their use of Safe2Tell®. One of the most important elements in the program's success is state legislation that protects the anonymity of the Safe2Tell® report. In 2007 the Colorado State Legislature enacted The Safe2Tell® Act, which guarantees the anonymity of all callers to Safe2Tell®. The assurance that calls cannot be traced and that appropriate action will be taken is critical to breaking the code of silence and helping young people to recognize that loyalty to friends sometimes means taking threats seriously and asking for help on their behalf. Safe2Tell® reports are also considered law enforcement intelligence information and are not to be included in case files or other public student records.

A second unique feature of the Safe2Tell® program is its training and educational outreach component. Individuals will not use Safe2Tell® unless they know about it and trust it. Publicizing the hotline and explaining how and when to use it is critical to its success. The training for students, teachers, administrators, bus drivers, and other staff stresses how to recognize a variety of common issues facing youth, as well as warning signs, threats to someone's safety, dangerous behavior, and unsafe situations. The training focuses on real-life scenarios, encouraging discussion and empowering youth to make a difference by speaking up, whether through Safe2Tell® anonymously or telling someone that would know how to intervene. Safe2Tell® provides protection from retribution and reassures young people that there will be follow-up. Importantly, the training emphasizes that the program provides a way to obtain help for a person that needs it.

An important goal is to present a strong but caring stance against the code of silence. A U.S. Secret Service study[3] found that if students think that telling the teacher about a dangerous situation will result only in punitive action against that individual, they are likely to keep it to themselves; if on the other hand, they believe that telling the teacher will result in that individual getting some help, they are more likely to report it. The goal of this training is to institutionalize Safe2Tell® within the school culture. It appears that this training is linked to higher levels of Safe2Tell®

use because of increased call volumes after student and staff presentations. Each presentation addresses the presence of the code of silence among our youth and how the Safe2Tell® program can break the code of silence by providing an anonymous way to report safety concerns and signs of dangerous behavior. The complete Safe2Tell® process is discussed in detail and both school and law enforcement are given ways to incorporate Safe2Tell® presentations and materials in their individual schools and communities.

There is also an intensive training component for state patrol personnel who answer Safe2Tell® calls. Communications officers receive training on a biannual basis that includes student issues, school culture issues, policy and procedure updates, technical support, and quality control. Also, monthly test calls are required and conducted by communications personnel. Relationship building and partnerships with schools and law enforcement help to create clear lines of communication between agencies. Outcome reports describing the individual event and outcome of that event are turned in to Safe2Tell® in a timely manner. There have been many positive statements praising the program effectiveness of Safe-2Tell® found directly on the outcome forms.

Implementation

Each community, district, or school has its own methods of promoting Safe2Tell®. Typical methods include printing Safe2Tell® information on the back of identification cards for staff, students, and parents, giving each student a bracelet with the phone number written on the inside, placing posters in the hallways or classrooms, and distributing a card for their wallet or purse. The card looks like a cell phone that opens up to reveal the ways to report to Safe2Tell®, along with reasons to call, tip, or text. There are also stickers, magnets, key fobs, and other marketing materials. Safe2Tell® makes available customized banners and signs for buses, and provides training at school-sponsored safety nights for parents.

On September 14, 2004, Safe2Tell® started taking calls. In each of the first two years, Safe2Tell® received about 100 tips. The number nearly tripled in the third year and increased to over 500 in the fourth year. The increase appears to be due to two factors: (1) public media attention after violent school incidents such as the Platte Canyon, Nickel Mines, and Virginia Tech shootings; and (2) widespread Safe2Tell® training in schools. Currently, operators receive over 100 calls a month. Since 2004, over 1,000 training sessions have occurred in Colorado schools and 500,000 pieces of informational material have been distributed. The system has handled 8,905 calls and processed 2,961 credible tip reports from 159 Colorado cities and fifty-six counties. There is wide support for implementing Safe2Tell® in the state. To be accredited with the Colorado Department of Education, schools must participate in the Safe2Tell® program and take new training classes every three years. In 2008 alone, training programs were conducted for more than 8,200 students, staff, and parents in eighty-eight schools.

Documenting Safe2Tell® effectiveness

Safe2Tell® has not been formally evaluated as a violence prevention program. There is some evidence of its effectiveness in the data collected on follow-up for tips received by Safe2Tell® and the tracking of responses of schools, law enforcement, and other agencies receiving referrals. These data suggest a positive impact of the Safe2Tell® program. Between September 2004 and November 2010, there was a wide range of reports regarding the following concerns: 782 bullying situations, 492 drug and alcohol incidents, 361 threats of violence, 210 guns or other weapons, 216 reports of harassment, 206 sexual misconduct events, 187 child-abuse incidents, 138 assaults, 111 fights, 102 cutting incidents, forty-nine gang-related activities, forty-two acts of vandalism, thirty-eight thefts, twenty-eight domestic violence incidents, eighteen sexting incidents, and thirteen events of animal cruelty. Follow-up data indicate that 83 percent of all Safe2Tell® incidents resulted in a positive intervention or action. These tips resulted in 415 formal investigations, 359 counseling referrals, 298 prevention/intervention plans, 324 potential suicide interventions, 312 school disciplinary actions, seventy-four arrests, and twenty-eight prevented school attacks. These results strongly suggest that the Safe2Tell® program has been successful in preventing school violence, although of course controlled studies are needed.

Although Safe2Tell® was developed as a violence prevention program, it appears to have had a positive impact on a broader range of student problems and concerns. It has resulted in interventions for potential suicide events, drug and alcohol abuse situations, the choking game (taking turns strangling each other to the point of getting lightheaded), and cutting (self-mutilation). We estimate that Safe2Tell® has prevented twenty-eight planned school attacks. The criteria for a prevented school attack include that the investigation resulted in the recovery of weapons and explosives (in one case, torturing devices), along with hit lists or letters of intent, and that law enforcement and school officials felt that an attack would likely have occurred had Safe2Tell® not been contacted and an investigation had not taken place. These attacks were reported by a variety of students, parents, teachers, administrators, and community members. Here are some examples of planned school attacks prevented through Safe2Tell®:

- A sixteen-year-old boy who attended a high school in the foothills west of Denver was arrested and convicted of illegal gun possession after a caller reported that his MySpace page showed photos of the teen posing with numerous guns, including rifles and handguns. The student had also written that several people deserved to die. The school expelled the teen and he was sent to a detention facility.
- A high school student from a small community in a Colorado eastern plains school told students he planned to "pull a Columbine." He gave the names of two fellow students he planned to kill, and disseminated a cell-phone video of himself with a shotgun saying he wanted "to kill some people." Because the report

came from a small town, numerous callers told Safe2Tell® operators that they were grateful for an anonymous way to report their concerns; they feared that if the student or his well-known family knew who had reported the teen, they could face retaliation.

• Another report stated that a boy from school was going to stab someone. He may have had a knife on him and possibly a second knife in his backpack. Both school and law enforcement were immediately notified by Safe2Tell®. The student's father was informed about the situation and was asked to bring his son in to talk with school administration. The father brought him in and said he did find two kitchen knives in his son's backpack. Upon further inspection, the suspect also had a razor blade in his pants pocket. The student was expelled for the rest of the school year and a law enforcement investigation was undertaken regarding the student's intent to harm other students.

There are many other cases that did not involve a plan to kill someone. For example:

• A student called Safe2Tell® to report that her friend posted to her Facebook page a description of cutting herself: "This feels good, it doesn't hurt as bad as I thought it would. If you do it fast enough you don't feel anything, just a little blood, no big deal." The student stated that her friend had cut herself in the past, but recently had started doing it again. Both law enforcement and the school received the Safe2Tell® report and followed up with the student. The school counselor was in contact with the student the next day at school and a therapy program was planned.

Future enhancements and dissemination plans

These case studies offer compelling evidence of the need for formal, scientific studies of the Safe2Tell® program to demonstrate its effectiveness. In the meantime, the program has attracted considerable attention by educators, law enforcement agencies, and policy makers. There are plans to expand and enhance the Safe2Tell® Web site to include conversation starters to facilitate the discussion of specific issues facing young people. There are also plans to provide downloadable posters and other resources. Production of a training video and a public-service announcement are planned next steps. There is also a higher education version being piloted in three Colorado community colleges. Other states and countries have expressed an interest in developing Safe2Tell® programs. The Safe2Tell® initiative empowers young people to share information that is potentially harmful or dangerous in a way that keeps them safe and anonymous and allows law enforcement and school officials to work together and intervene early, ultimately preventing violence and saving lives.

Notes

1. Erickson, W. (2001). *The report of Governor Bill Owens' Columbine Review Commission*. Denver, CO: The State of Colorado.
2. U.S. Secret Service & U.S. Department of Education. (2004). *Final report and findings of the Safe School Initiative*. Washington, DC: U.S. Department of Education.
3. U.S. Secret Service & U.S. Department of Education. (2004). *Threat assessment in schools: A guide to managing threatening situations and to creating safe school climates*. Washington, DC: U.S. Department of Education.

SUSAN R. T. PAYNE *is a special agent with the Colorado Office of the Attorney General and director of the Safe2Tell® Program, located in the Colorado Attorney General's Office.*

DELBERT S. ELLIOTT *is the director of the Center for the Study and Prevention of Violence in the Institute of Behavioral Science at the University of Colorado, Boulder.*

Developmental research on social influences can guide practices aimed to prevent homicidal youth violence.

8

Recurrent issues in efforts to prevent homicidal youth violence in schools: Expert opinions

Karen E. Dill, Richard E. Redding,
Peter K. Smith, Ray Surette, Dewey G. Cornell

THE PURPOSE OF THIS ARTICLE is to consider four issues that are raised repeatedly by public policy makers, educators, and juvenile justice authorities in seeking ways to prevent youth violence in general and homicidal attacks on schools in particular. The first topic, bullying, has received great attention because many youth involved in school shootings and other violent attacks at school have been victims of bullying (although the severity of the bullying has been variable). The two boys who carried out the Columbine shootings cast themselves as champions of victims of bullying in their videos and writings, some still available on the Internet.[1] Although there are undoubtedly more complex motives and goals behind their crime, they left the impression, amplified by media

Coauthors Dill, Redding, Smith, and Surette made comparable contributions to this manuscript and are listed in alphabetical order. Cornell was the organizing author for this article.

reports, that their attack was an act of protest against bullies, school authorities, and society in general. Youth around the world who identified with this cause, and who projected onto the Columbine shootings that it represented action against the kind of injustices they experienced, found it to be a source of encouragement for their own plans. For this reason, it is important to consider the role that anti-bullying programs might play in the prevention of school shootings.

The second topic concerns the influence of entertainment violence, especially violent video games and music. Few topics have generated as much debate and controversy over the past fifty years as research on the effects of violent media on children's behavior and development.[2] The fact that the Columbine youth, as well as youth involved in several other high-profile cases, were known as ardent players of video games that rewarded rampage killing of as many opponents as possible has added a new depth of concern to this topic.

The third topic concerns the generation of copycat crimes by news media reports of sensational acts of violence. Notably, the Columbine boys aspired to achieve infamy by far exceeding the violent impact attained by previous school shooters and, in turn, the unprecedented news coverage of their crime has shaped the actions of other youth who made references to Columbine in their threats or plans to carry out similar acts.

The fourth topic concerns the possible role of deterrence through tougher criminal penalties for juvenile offenders. Policy makers frequently question whether potential offenders might be deterred through more serious criminal sanctions. Perhaps there could be a deterrent effect on some youth who contemplate homicidal acts of violence at school, as well as those who engage in bullying and harassment that might precipitate such acts. For those youth who have decided to kill themselves as part of their attack, deterrence may seem moot. However, a society that holds juvenile offenders more accountable for their actions could experience a generalized effect on attitudes toward criminal behavior that might yield some protective influence.

NEW DIRECTIONS FOR YOUTH DEVELOPMENT • DOI: 10.1002/yd

Four leading experts on these topics responded to the question: "What are the most promising findings in your field in the past ten years that can help us prevent homicidal violence by students in schools?"

Bullying prevention

Bullying refers to intentional aggressive acts where there is repetition and an imbalance of power. Being a victim can contribute, independently of other factors, to mental health problems such as self-harm and psychotic symptoms.[3] Although the causal direction is less certain, we also know that homicidal violence by students often appears to be associated with claims of being bullied.[4] Thus, research on bullying prevention is likely to be relevant to prevention of homicidal violence in school.

Neighborhood, school, classroom, peer group, and family factors have all been implicated as associated with bullying rates.[5,6] The school and class climate, and the extent to which schools implement effective school anti-bullying policies and other interventions, are generally held to be important. The impact of family factors appears relatively small, but may be more important for students involved in homicidal violence, for whom family-based interventions may also be indicated.[7]

However, schools can make a difference. Over the last fifteen years, many anti-bullying school-based interventions have been developed, and recent meta-analyses suggest that they generally have some degree of success.[8] Besides having a clear and accessible written policy, schools can implement proactive and reactive strategies. Proactive strategies develop a school climate of responsibility and (in Spanish) *convivencia*—being able to get along together. These include curriculum activities, such as use of DVDs, drama, quality circles, education for citizenship and social and emotional aspects of learning, incorporating learning goals (for example, respect for others) and ways of doing this (for example, cooperative group work). Assertiveness training can benefit all pupils but especially those at risk of being victims.

Peer support schemes, such as buddying, mentoring, and running lunchtime clubs, involve other students (often a year or so older) in helping with problems that may include peer relationship issues and bullying. As emphasized in the recent KiVa project in Finland, it is important that peer supporters are not only well trained and supported, but that they are themselves respected or high status in the peer-group community. One of the motives for bullying appears to be gaining peer-group status, and the peer group itself can challenge this, but effectively only if high-status peers act as defenders of the victim.[7]

There are also reactive strategies that range from direct sanctions (for example, detention, exclusion) to counseling approaches in which the perpetrator is not sanctioned but asked to change his or her behavior. Restorative approaches take a middle route, holding perpetrators responsible for their actions but seeking to restore workable relationships. More research is needed on the relative effectiveness of these strategies,[9] but many schools use a flexible tailored response, moving from restorative approaches to more direct sanctions if needed.

Traditional bullying can be physical, verbal, or indirect (for example, rumor spreading). Over the last ten years, cyberbullying has emerged in a variety of formats, such as mobile phones and the Internet. Rates appear to be up to about one-third of all bullying. Some cyberbullies appear to be particularly disturbed children (maybe traditional bully/victims—students who are perpetrators as well as victims of bullying) who use cyberspace as a way of obtaining revenge on those they feel have attacked them. Given that homicidally violent students often act out of anger, shame, acute or chronic social rejection, and a desire to make a public statement by posting violent Internet material, this area may be especially relevant.[10] Efforts to reduce cyberbullying have been attempted in many countries, although the area is not yet very well researched and interventions are less developed than for traditional bullying.[11]

Video game and entertainment violence

The Columbine shooters were reportedly avid players of the first-person shooter video game *Doom*, prompting questions about the role of video games and other entertainment media in school shootings. The overarching conclusion from dozens of studies is that video games are effective teaching tools, but their lessons can be positive or negative.

In 2003, a team of top media violence scholars concluded that "the debate over whether media violence increases aggression and violence is essentially over...."[12] Analysis of research from a variety of genres, including video games, television, movies, and music, revealed that media violence exposure increases the likelihood of aggression and violence in youth. Attractive media models of aggression and identification with characters increase the aggression-provoking effect.[13]

Brain research has begun to elucidate the relationship between media violence and aggression. For example, Bartholow, Bushman, and Sestir[14] found that violent video game players showed reduced empathic sensitivity, as measured by nERPs (negative event-related potentials) when watching scenes of real-life violence as compared to controls. Moreover, heavy users of violent video games were significantly more aggressive than the light users in a laboratory aggression task.

Despite the large body of evidence, public understanding of media violence is hampered by some common media violence myths.[15] For example, parents, government officials, and other stakeholders may mistakenly believe that media effects are simple, direct, and extreme; that they affect all people the same way; and that exposure to media violence always leads to immediate effects.[16] Actually, media effects are likely to be more complex and subtle. For example, consequences of exposure may build over time and lead to more everyday forms of aggression such as insults and sexual harassment, as well as reduced helping behavior.[17] Scientists are currently modeling media violence effects with the use of risk factor approaches. Risk factor models, as in medicine, are probabilistic and therefore can help us avoid misconceptions such as the idea that every exposure to media violence results in violence or aggression.[18]

In the groups most commonly studied in psychological research, media violence effects may be stronger for milder forms of aggression than for extreme forms of violence.[12] Therefore, studies focusing on everyday aggression as a consequence of exposure to media violence may help attenuate some of the media violence myths. In one such study, Dill and colleagues[19] found that exposure to demeaning portrayals of female game characters caused increased tolerance of sexual harassment for male, but not female, college students.

In recent years, attention has turned to video games as powerful teachers. Gentile and Gentile[20] note, for instance, that games have clear objectives, promote active learning and overlearning, teach mastery with the use of multiple contexts, use progressive levels of difficulty, and offer varied rewards (à la operant conditioning).

Although research has demonstrated that learning can take the form of aggression, games also have the potential to teach positive lessons.[20] In previous years, the majority of top-selling video games and children's favorite games have been violent,[21,22] but there are some new trends; nonviolent games, particularly music and exercise games, have become increasingly popular. Also in recent years, a serious games movement has arisen with emphases on political activism, health-related games, and educational games.

Although there has been a tendency to impose a false dichotomy that video games are either good or bad, this black-and-white thinking is counterproductive and inaccurate. Game effects depend on a variety of factors, such as content, time spent playing, and individual differences.[23]

News reports and copycat crimes

Copycat crime is a phenomenon in which media coverage of a crime generates subsequent similar crimes. Copycat effects are thought to have a significant influence on criminally predisposed youth, and to have contributed to some incidents of school violence. Rigorous empirical studies of copycat crime are rare, and most evidence consists of anecdotal reports. However, sound empirical research has linked media coverage to copycat suicides among teenagers.[24] Coleman[25] provides an extensive list of copycat phenomena such as teenage cluster suicides, airplane hijackings, and school shootings. For school shootings, copycat threats far outnumber actual copycat events.[26]

There is indirect support for youth copycat effects in research on social diffusion (how behaviors spread through societies), imitation (how individuals come to copy behavior), priming (mental processes that encourage copying), and social learning (how individuals learn behaviors in social settings), as well as media behavioral effects research. Surette[27] and Hurley and Chater[28] provide overviews of copycat crime and human copycat behavior suggesting that the media accounts most likely to generate copycat crimes: (1) show successful, unpunished, justified crimes committed by heroic models; (2) show crime in realistic settings and as exciting and enjoyable; (3) minimize or justify the harm caused by crime; and (4) include clear and explicit crime instructions. Individual characteristics that may increase a youth's risk of copycat behavior include (1) social isolation, (2) stronger networking to deviant than law-abiding groups, (3) high interest in criminogenic media content or a specific generator crime, (4) belief in personal criminal innovativeness and efficacy, (5) interest in guns and law enforcement activities, or (6) feelings of persecution and anger.

Two hypothesized risk factors linked to homicidal copycat events are media immersion—when individuals concentrate for hours on a single media product or story—and fixation—when individuals repetitively watch the same scene and adopt similar mannerisms, clothing, or speech patterns.[29] However, none of the hypothesized risk factors has demonstrated strong predictive value and none can be regarded as necessary or sufficient to lead to copycat behavior.

Contemporary media are not monolithic. News and entertainment are today fused as "infotainment" and news media content is no longer restricted to news outlets. Additionally, new media, such as PDAs, iPods, and YouTube, are likely more influential on youth than traditional newspapers and television media. Thus, news media effects cannot be easily parsed out. Finally, research on other types of media effects suggests that interventions need to be carefully implemented to avoid counterproductive results.[30] With these caveats in mind, some recommendations can be made.

Prevention efforts should focus on encouraging the news media to avoid criminogenic media content before a major crime occurs. Crime reports should avoid accounts that glorify or justify the crime, or provide instruction to potential copycats. Schools might reduce at-risk copycat populations through a combination of media and criminal justice literacy instruction that debunks misperceptions about crime. Youth often have mistaken perceptions of the criminal justice system, their real-world risk of apprehension, and the consequences of criminal acts. Thus, even when the initial offenders are shown in the news as unsuccessful, at-risk copycat youth will interpret this to mean that the initial offenders made correctable mistakes that can be avoided by the copycat, resulting in successfully copied crimes. Proactive steps are strongly recommended before newsworthy violent events occur and should be reinforced following one.

To minimize copycat effects after a potential generator crime, the first step is to open discussions and contextualize the event for youth. The criminogenic media portrait can be defused by (1) pointing out inconsistent and speculative content regarding the initial crime; (2) discussing the crime's true aftermath, so that victims are portrayed sympathetically and offenders are viewed negatively and denied folk hero status; (3) discussions of alternative, more appropriate actions the initial offenders could have pursued; (4) discussing the high likelihood of failure, arrest, and punishment for similar crimes as well as the negative consequences for family, friends, and future of copycat offenders.

Lastly, as soon as feasible, communities should minimize social disruptions such as closing schools and holding memorials that keep the initial crime and offenders in the spotlight. It is important for a school to return to normal as soon as it is safe to do so to reduce the lure of copying an act simply to replicate and continue long-term social upheaval. As soon as it is deemed safe, schools should resume normal schedules and routines. And to the degree possible, news agencies should be asked to limit visual images, perpetrator-focused content, perpetrator statements or interviews, extended coverage, and comparisons to past infamous persons.

The effectiveness of deterrence

The question often arises as to whether more punitive sanctions for juvenile crime can prevent homicidal violence. For adult offenders, the research suggests that the likelihood of arrest acts as a deterrent, whereas the severity of the punishment does not. The fewer studies involving juveniles (none of which has focused on school homicides), briefly reviewed below, reach similar conclusions (see Redding[31]).

In the wake of legal reforms in the United States designed to get tough on juvenile crime by transferring juveniles from the juvenile court to the adult criminal court, recent research has examined the differential effects of trying serious youthful offenders in juvenile versus criminal court. The research has generally found that the stiffer adult sanctions do not deter juvenile crime. For comprehensive reviews, see McGowan and others[32] and Redding.[31] Studies have controlled for demographic and economic variables and compared the juvenile arrest rates across states as a function of whether they had particular transfer laws in place, or as a function of the relative punitiveness of the sentences given in their juvenile and criminal justice systems. Other studies have compared offending rates before and after a state enacted or strengthened transfer laws, and one study examined the effect of reaching the age of majority on youthful offending. Only one of these studies found a general deterrent effect. A recent small-scale study[33] that interviewed transferred juvenile offenders found that few knew they could be tried as adults, none thought it would happen to them, and few thought they would face serious punishment. Most thought they would get light sentences from the juvenile court despite the serious violent crimes they had committed.

Punishments will likely have deterrent effects only if potential offenders believe there is a high likelihood of getting caught and of receiving a meaningfully significant sentence, and only if they consider the risk of the penalty when deciding whether to offend. Some adolescents may have difficulty perceiving the risk of being arrested and punished because of their psychosocial and brain immaturity, their susceptibility to peer pressure, and their tendency to focus on the short-term benefits of crime while discounting the consequences of their actions (see Beckman[34] and Steinberg and Cauffman[35]). In addition, school shootings are unusual crimes that may be committed by suicidal youth with little or no prior history of offending, which further suggests that the prospect of punishment would have little deterrent effect.

Six large-scale studies have also found higher recidivism rates among juveniles convicted of violent offenses in criminal court when compared with similar offenders tried in the juvenile court.[31,32] These studies used large sample sizes, multiple measures of recidivism, and different study design and analysis methods; they controlled for a variety of variables (for example, age, race, prior offenses, offense seriousness, use of a weapon, geographical location, family status, case-processing variables) and were conducted in different states of the United States. The higher recidivism rates may be due to stigmatization and labeling effects, the sense of injustice juveniles report feeling about being tried as adults, the learning of criminal attitudes, exposure to victimization while incarcerated with adults, the decreased focus on rehabilitation and family support in the adult system, and decreased opportunities for community reintegration.[32] In contrast, incarceration in the juvenile justice system, with its availability of rehabilitative programming, may have beneficial effects in reducing recidivism.[31,36]

In sum, because the extant research suggests that harsher criminal penalties do not prevent juvenile violence, there is no reason to suppose that they would prevent homicidal violence in schools. Instead, we must devote the resources necessary to detect and arrest those juveniles who engage in violent acts.[37] More importantly, we must utilize the available evidence-based treatments to prevent delinquent behavior and reduce recidivism. We now know what works (particularly cognitive–behavioral and family-based treatments, and interpersonal skills training) versus what does not work (punishment, boot camps, shock incarceration) in treating and preventing serious juvenile delinquency. Such treatments have proven highly effective, particularly when started at the first sign of significant conduct disorder or delinquent behavior and delivered in a high-quality fashion.[38]

Conclusions

Case studies suggest that the pathway to a school shooting develops over a long period of time, and that childhood problems were often evident years before the attack. Therefore, prevention efforts might be arrayed along a continuum from the earliest manifestations of developmental difficulty through the period of conception, planning, and ultimate decision to act.

Adolescents normatively and characteristically grow markedly less dependent on their parents for guidance and support, and instead turn toward peers as the source for feelings of acceptance, identity, and self-worth. Under normal conditions this developmental shift can be regarded as an adaptive preparation for adult independence. Research on youth who have committed homicidal attacks at school seems to suggest a developmental failure along this normal adolescent trajectory.[39] Many of these youth had excessively attenuated ties with their parents that were compounded by failure to attain acceptance with their primary peer group. They experienced bullying, teasing, or other forms of peer rejection. These experiences, perhaps in combination with other social and academic failures, left them with profound feelings of depression, alienation, narcissistic injury, resentment, and anger.

Although there may be no reliable way to determine which students will be so profoundly affected by bullying, schoolwide efforts to address bullying, as well as efforts to identify and assist students who seem seriously troubled, could be helpful. It must be emphasized that early prevention efforts at a universal level can be effective even when there is no means of determining which members of the general population are destined to develop long-term negative effects. Similarly, an entire nation might be vaccinated against a disease that would otherwise affect only a small proportion of the population.

Clearly only a few youth are so vulnerable to the impact of peer rejection that they would consider a homicidal attack as a public act of revenge, so there must be other factors (and likely different combinations of factors in each case) that influence them in their progression toward violence. Among these other factors may be the desensitizing effect of entertainment violence on inhibitions against harming others and the suggestive effect of sensational media coverage of school shootings. These factors are certainly not necessary or sufficient causes of violence, but they are noteworthy because they are extraordinarily pervasive public influences that are increasingly embedded in cultures throughout the world and can occupy large quantities of the adolescent's daily life. Their distorting impact on the legitimacy of violence may be greatest on those who are most troubled and in need of time spent in more constructive and reparative activities. There are clear directions for ameliorating their impact.

Finally, research on the deterrent effects of criminal sanctions on youth provides strong counsel against reliance on harsher punishment as a readily available and easily implemented preventive measure. Often it is politically popular to recommend tougher criminal sanctions, but rehabilitative treatment efforts offer scientifically more persuasive evidence of effectiveness.

Notes

1. Columbine Review Commission. (2001). *The report of Governor Bill Owens' Columbine Review Commission.* Denver, CO: State of Colorado.
2. Bushman, B. J., & Anderson, C. A. (2001). Media violence and the American public: Scientific facts versus media misinformation. *American Psychologist, 56,* 477–489.
3. Arsenault, L., Bowes, L., & Shakoor, S. (2009). Bullying victimization in youths and mental health problems: "Much ado about nothing"? *Psychological Medicine, 29,* 1–13.
4. Reuter-Rice, K. (2008). Male adolescent bullying and the school shooter. *Journal of School Nursing, 24,* 350–359.
5. Bowes, L., Arsenault, L., Maughan, B., Taylor, A., Caspi, A., & Moffitt, T. E. (2009). School, neighborhood, and family factors are associated with children's bullying involvement: A nationally representative longitudinal study. *Journal of the American Academy of Child and Adolescent Psychiatry, 48,* 545–553.
6. Salmivalli, C. (2010). Bullying and the peer group: A review. *Aggression and Violent Behavior, 15,* 112–120.
7. Curtner-Smith, M. E., Smith, P. K., & Porter, M. (2010). Family level intervention with bullies and victims. In E. Vernberg & B. Biggs (Eds.), *Preventing and treating bullying and victimization* (pp. 177–193). New York: Oxford University Press.
8. Farrington, D. P., & Ttofi, M. M. (2009). Reducing school bullying: Evidence-based implications for policy. *Crime and Justice, 38,* 281–345.
9. Burssens, D., & Vettenburg, N. (2006). Restorative group conferencing at school: A constructive response to serious incidents. *Journal of School Violence, 5,* 5–17.
10. Leary, M. R., Kowalski, R. M., Smith, L., & Phillips, S. (2003). Teasing, rejection, and violence: Case studies of the school shootings. *Aggressive Behavior, 29,* 202–214.
11. Mishna, F., Cook, C., Saini, M., Wu, M. J., & MacFadden, R. (2009). Interventions for children, youth and parents to prevent and reduce cyber abuse. *Campbell Systematic Reviews, 2.*
12. Anderson, C. A., Berkowitz, L., Donnerstein, E., Huesmann, L. R., Johnson, J. D., Linz, D., et al. (2003). The influence of media violence on youth. *Psychological Science in the Public Interest, 4,* 81–110.
13. Huesmann, L. R., Moise-Titus, J., Podolski, C. L., & Eron, L. D. (2003). Longitudinal relations between children's exposure to TV violence and their aggressive and violent behavior in young adulthood: 1977–1992. *Developmental Psychology, 39,* 201–221.
14. Bartholow, B. D., Bushman, B. J., & Sestir, M. A. (2006). Chronic violent video game exposure and desensitization to violence: Behavioral and event-related brain potential data. *Journal of Experimental Social Psychology, 42,* 532–539.
15. Gentile, D., & Sesma, A. (2003). Developmental approaches to understanding media effects on individuals. In D. Gentile (Ed.), *Media violence and children* (pp. 19–37). Westport, CT: Praeger.

16. Potter, W. J. (2002). *The eleven myths of media violence.* Thousand Oaks, CA: Sage.

17. Bushman, B. J., & Anderson, C. A. (2009). Comfortably numb: Desensitizing effects of violent media on helping others. *Psychological Science, 20,* 273–277.

18. Anderson, C. A., Gentile, D. A., & Buckley, K. E. (2007). *Violent video game effects on children and adolescents: Theory, research, and public policy.* New York: Oxford University Press.

19. Dill, K. E., Brown, B. P., & Collins, M. A. (2008). Effects of exposure to sex-stereotyped video game characters on tolerance of sexual harassment. *Journal of Experimental Social Psychology, 44,* 1402–1408.

20. Gentile, D. A., & Gentile, J. R. (2008). Video games as exemplary teachers: A conceptual analysis. *Journal of Youth and Adolescence, 37,* 127–141.

21. Dill, K. E., Gentile, D. A., Richter, W. A., & Dill, J. C. (2005). Violence, sex, age and race in popular video games: A content analysis. In E. Cole & J. Henderson-Daniel (Eds.), *Featuring females: Feminist analyses of media* (pp. 115–130). Washington, DC: American Psychological Association.

22. Funk, J. B., & Buchman, D. D. (1996). Children's perceptions of gender differences in social approval for playing electronic games. *Sex Roles, 35,* 219–231.

23. Dill, K. E. (2009). *How fantasy becomes reality: Seeing through media influence.* New York: Oxford University Press.

24. Phillips, D., & Carstensen, L. (1986). Clustering of teenage suicides after television news stories about suicide. *New England Journal of Medicine, 315,* 685–689.

25. Coleman, L. (2004). *The copycat effect.* New York: Paraview.

26. Kostinsky, S., Bixlwer, E., & Kettl, P. (2001). Threats of school violence in Pennsylvania after media coverage of the Columbine High School massacre. *Archives Pediatric Adolescent Medicine, 155,* 994–1001.

27. Surette, R. (2010). *Media, crime, and criminal justice.* Belmont, CA: Thomson.

28. Hurley, S., & Chater, N. (2005). *Perspectives on imitation.* Cambridge, MA: MIT Press.

29. Meloy, J. R., & Mohandie, K. (2001). Investigating the role of screen violence in specific homicide cases. *Journal of Forensic Science, 46,* 1113–1118.

30. Sacco, V., & Silverman, R. (1982). Selling crime prevention: The evaluation of a mass media campaign. *Canadian Journal of Criminology, 23,* 191–201.

31. Redding, R. E. (2008). *Juvenile transfer laws: An effective deterrent to delinquency?* Juvenile Justice Bulletin NCJ-220595. Washington, DC: U.S. Department of Justice.

32. McGowan, A., Hahn, R., Liberman, A., Crosby, A., Fullilove, M., Johnson, R., et al. (2007). Effects on violence of laws and policies facilitating the transfer of juveniles from the juvenile system to the adult system. *American Journal of Preventive Medicine, 32,* S7–S28.

33. Redding, R. E., & Fuller, E. J. (2004, Summer). What do juvenile offenders know about being tried as adults? Implications for deterrence. *Juvenile & Family Court Journal*, 35–45.

34. Beckman, M. (2004). Crime, culpability, and the adolescent brain. *Science*, *305*, 596–599.

35. Steinberg, L., & Cauffman, E. (1996). Maturity of judgment in adolescence: Psychosocial factors in adolescent decision making. *Law & Human Behavior*, *20*, 249–272.

36. Hjalmarsson, R. (2009). Juvenile jails: A path to the straight and narrow or to hardened criminality? *Journal of Law and Economics*, *52*, 779–809.

37. Redding, R. E., & Shalf, S. M. (2001). The legal context of school violence: Effectiveness of federal, state, and local law enforcement efforts to reduce gun violence in schools. *Law & Policy*, *23*, 297–343.

38. Heilbrun, K., Goldstein, N. E. S., & Redding, R. E. (Eds.). (2005). *Juvenile delinquency: Prevention, assessment, and intervention*. New York: Oxford University Press.

39. Cornell, D. (2006). *School violence: Fears versus facts.* Mahwah, NJ: Lawrence Erlbaum; Moore, M. H., Petrie, C. V., Braga, A. A., & McLaughlin, B. L. (Eds.). (2003). *Deadly lessons: Understanding lethal school violence*. Washington, DC: National Academies Press; O'Toole, M. E. (2000). *The school shooter: A threat assessment perspective.* Quantico, VA: National Center for the Analysis of Violent Crime, Federal Bureau of Investigation; Vossekuil, B., Fein, R. A., Reddy, M., Borum, R., & Modzeleski, W. (2002). *The final report and findings of the Safe School Initiative: Implications for the prevention of school attacks in the United States.* Washington, DC: U.S. Secret Service and U.S. Department of Education; Bondü et al., this issue.

KAREN E. DILL *is the director of the first doctoral program in media psychology in the United States at Fielding Graduate University in Santa Barbara, California, and the author of* How Fantasy Becomes Reality.

RICHARD E. REDDING *is associate dean and professor at Chapman University School of Law in California. He has written extensively on juvenile justice, particularly sentencing policy and rehabilitation programs for serious juvenile offenders.*

PETER K. SMITH *is professor of psychology and head of the Unit for School and Family Studies at Goldsmiths, University of London, United Kingdom. He has researched extensively on school bullying, and is chair of COST Action IS0801 on Cyberbullying (2008–2012).*

RAY SURETTE *is professor of Criminal Justice in the College of Health and Public Affairs at the University of Central Florida.*

DEWEY G. CORNELL *is professor of education in the Programs in Clinical and School Psychology of the Curry School of Education at the University of Virginia.*

Index

Other Titles Available

people who fall off the graduation path are more prone than ever before to experience chronic unemployment, poverty, ill health, dependence on social welfare, and a lifetime of struggle. The enormous costs to these individuals, their communities, and our society call on us to invest in systems that accurately identify young people at risk of dropping out of school and provide the supports necessary to keep them on track to graduation. This issue offers perspectives and strategies for engaging American youth in learning, keeping them on the graduation path, and preparing them for success in college and career. The ideas, practices, and programs set out in this volume advance innovations in such areas as using data to identify and support at-risk youth; pedagogical approaches and technology that motivate youth to learn; organizing and resourcing schools, school systems, and partnerships to support every student; and galvanizing communities and our nation around creating responsive, aligned, and effective educational opportunities for all youth.
ISBN: 978-047093322-0

YD126   **Play, Talk, Learn: Promising Practices in Youth Mentoring**
Michael J. Karcher, Michael J. Nakkula
This volume brings together the findings from separate studies of community-based and school-based mentoring to unpack the common response to the question of what makes youth mentoring work. A debate that was alive in 2002, when the first *New Directions for Youth Development* volume on mentoring, edited by Jean Rhodes, was published, centers on whether goal-oriented or relationship-focused interactions (conversations and activities) prove to be more essential for effective youth mentoring. The consensus appeared then to be that the mentoring context defined the answer: in workplace mentoring with teens, an instrumental relationship was deemed essential and resulted in larger impacts, while in the community setting, the developmental relationship was the key ingredient of change. Recent large-scale studies of school-based mentoring have raised this question once again and suggest that understanding how developmental and instrumental relationship styles manifest through goal-directed and relational interactions is essential to effective practice. Because the contexts in which youth mentoring occurs (in the community, in school during the day, or in a structured program after school) affect what happens in the mentor-mentee pair, our goal was to bring together a diverse group of researchers to describe the focus, purpose, and authorship of the mentoring interactions that happen in these contexts in order to help mentors and program staff better understand how youth mentoring relationships can be effective.
ISBN: 978-0-470-88006-7

YD125 **Cultural Agents and Creative Arts**
Doris Sommer, Andrés Sanín
When youth engage in creative arts, they become authors of new works and experience the possibilities of exercising the power of their own creative and critical thinking. Art is "symbolic destruction"; it provides constructive outlets for normal aggressivity and vehicles for exploring the world. More than modes of expression, artistic media are also engaging modes of interpretation and learning. The cultural agents whom we feature here are models who can inspire more instructors and facilitators to promote youth development by sharing particular artistic training and anticipating rigorous results. The goal of this volume is to inspire practitioners, advocates, policy professionals, and researchers interested in youth development through exemplary cases of art that has stimulated positive change in youth and in their general communities. Each case proposes novel scholarly and artistic projects for nonviolent social change, with the belief that creativity is vital to the health of democracies and that it is critical to the development of ethical, socially engaged, and resourceful citizens among our youth.
ISBN 978-0-470-63384-7

YD124 **Framing Youth Development for Public Support**
Lynn Davey
Since 1999, the nonprofit FrameWorks Institute has investigated how Americans think about social issues—from children and youth to education and race—and how scientists, policy experts, and advocates can do a better job of engaging the public in solutions. FrameWorks Institute's empirical approach integrates essential constructs from the cognitive and social sciences to investigate the worldviews and patterns of thinking that ordinary people enlist when considering social problems. The goal of this approach is to deliver communications strategies that are grounded in research and have the potential to change the public debate if they are effectively deployed. This volume focuses on the theory, research, and practice of FrameWorks' decade of work in evidence-based communications strategies for child and youth issues. The articles explain where this approach is situated within the broader conversation on communications for social change; why an iterative, multimethod process is necessary to determine the communications strategies that will elevate the public dimensions of children's and youth's developmental trajectories; and how experts and advocates are applying these evidence-based communications strategies to their work on behalf of children and youth.
ISBN 978-04706-04199

YD123 **Youth in Participatory Action Research**
Tara M. Brown, Louie F. Rodríguez
Youth from historically marginalized groups in the United States face a host of problems that threaten their well-being now and in the future, including inadequate formal education, disproportionate

punishment by schools and law enforcement, poverty, family insta-
bility, and exposure to guns, violence, and illegal drugs. Public
schools, social services, and other social systems intended to address
these problems have struggled to transform the lives of these
young people on a broad scale. The authors in this volume of *New
Directions for Youth Development* take an innovative approach to
addressing the difficulties that marginalized youth face. They
engage young people in investigations of and interventions into
their everyday challenges through participatory action research. In
doing so, they demonstrate and nurture the tremendous capacity of
young people to both understand and transform the conditions of
their lives in ways that move toward social equity and justice.
ISBN 978-04705-76953

YD122   **Universities in Partnership: Strategies for Education, Youth
        Development, and Community Renewal**
        Ira Harkavy, Matthew Hartley
        Over the past two decades, a democratic, engaged civic university
        movement has developed across the United States. A central feature
        of this movement has been university-community partnerships in
        which higher education institutions work with organizations and
        schools in their local community. Much of this work has focused on
        the education and development of young people. Over time, signifi-
        cant change has occurred regarding both the quantity and quality of
        partnerships, and intriguing models have been developed. Five uni-
        versity-community partnerships from across the United States are
        featured in this volume. Each has been developed over a number of
        years and has focused on making a genuine difference in the condition
        of young people and their schools and communities. The case studies
        are from the State University of New York, Buffalo; Indiana Univer-
        sity-Purdue University Indianapolis; University of Pennsylvania;
        University of Dayton; and Widener University. Each demonstrates
        that university-school-community partnerships have the capacity to
        build communities, advance democracy, and enhance the quality of
        life and learning for all Americans, particularly its children.
        ISBN 978-04705-29836

YD121   **Defining and Measuring Quality in Youth Programs and
        Classrooms**
        Nicole Yohalem, Robert C. Granger, Karen J. Pittman
        In this volume, scholars who study three different settings—class-
        rooms, youth programs, and mentoring dyads—reflect on what con-
        stitutes quality in their setting and how to think about measuring it.
        The authors focus specifically on quality "at the point of service,"
        meaning the specific practices, processes, and interactions that
        occur among adults and youth in the setting. The articles also offer
        practical advice about effective and manageable ways that practi-
        tioners can incorporate assessment into their work in order to

improve quality. Together these articles represent a wealth of knowledge about what is important to measure in youth-serving settings and the pros and cons of different approaches to measurement. This information can help practitioners and policymakers grapple with how to use scarce evaluation resources wisely, establish productive accountability systems, and link data and program improvement strategies in ways that make services more effective.
ISBN 978-04704-87518

YD120   **Where Youth Development Meets Mental Health and Education: The RALLY Approach**
Tina Malti, Gil G. Noam
This volume focuses on the RALLY (Responsive Advocacy for Life and Learning in Youth) approach, which integrates youth development, mental health, and education for young people in middle schools and after-school programs. RALLY is designed to give students the integrated systems of support they need to thrive and succeed. The approach is built on developmental and relational principles and emphasizes a risk and resilience framework. For a decade, it has built a preventive framework and an early intervention practice that never feels to the youth as receiving services. A new developmentalist role, the RALLY practitioner, helps to implement youth development principles in schools and connects students' often fractured and diverse worlds, including family and community. This issue is relevant for all teachers, administrators, student support staff, after-school providers, youth workers, and mental health and health professionals.
ISBN 978-04704-67206

YD119   **Youth, Violence, and Social Disintegration**
Wilhelm Heitmeyer, Sandra Legge
How and why do people become perpetrators and victims of violence? In youth violence, what roles are played by public spaces, the institutional context, socialization processes, religion and other kinds of ideologies, and, more generally, the experience of social disintegration? Are there global commonalities with regard to programs for preventing and intervening in youth crime? A look at the global trends of youth crime and violence and the development of social conditions for young people worldwide shows the importance of finding answers to these questions. This volume examines violent behavior and addresses these questions in an international context. The theoretical framework for all of the articles is the theory of disintegration. The article authors examine whether the disintegration approach, which suggests that social disintegration encourages the development of socially harmful attitudes and behavior, offers explanations for the forms of youth violence under examination and for the experience of violence.
ISBN 978-04704-24094

YD118   **Spiritual Development**
Peter L. Benson, Eugene C. Roehlkepartain, Kathryn L. Hong
The past decade has seen an explosion in interest in spiritual development within youth development and related fields. National youth-serving systems are beginning to ask how they can effectively address this issue in a society that has become increasingly diverse and pluralistic. Drawing on the global research and field-building efforts of Search Institute's Center for Spiritual Development in Childhood and Adolescence, this volume of *New Directions for Youth Development* frames a new, deeper dialogue about the intersections between youth development and spiritual development. Its contributors explore ways to integrate spiritual development and youth development in order to strengthen theory, research, and practice.
ISBN 978-04703-90801

YD117   **Community Organizing and Youth Advocacy**
Sarah Deschenes, Milbrey Mclaughlin, Anne Newman
This issue presents new thinking about the ways in which youth and parents are engaged in local reform, particularly education reform, with the help of community organizations. Community groups examined in this volume advocate for and with youth in a variety of ways: through youth organizing, parent organizing, more traditional youth advocacy, and funding support. There is a ripple effect in these local efforts; not only do policies and political contexts change, but individual and communities themselves begin to change too. And although there are significant barriers to changing entrenched ideas about youth and their needs, the efforts discussed in these articles are having tangible results in many urban areas.
ISBN 978-04703-43616

YD116   **Afterschool Around the Globe: Policy, Practices, and Youth Voice**
Jen Hilmer Capece, Andrew Schneider-Muñoz, Bonnie Politz
Afterschool presents in a variety of forms across the globe. This developmental time, variously referred to as afterschool, out-of-school-time, or free time, can range from workforce preparation for twenty-year-olds in South Africa to safe spaces and healthy activities for eight-year-olds in New Zealand. Sponsored by the National AfterSchool Association, the global contributors to this issue share knowledge and commitment to effective afterschool efforts. They focus on meaningful youth participation in a wide variety of venues and settings. Building global citizens, giving youth an economic edge, and combining self-interest and learning are some of the underlying outcomes described throughout this volume. It draws out lessons learned across cultural and geographical borders and addresses significant policies and quality standards.
ISBN 978-0-470-28239-7